The Ecological Constitutio

The Ecological Constitution integrates the insights of environmental constitutionalism and ecological law in a concise, engaging and accessible manner.

This book sets out the necessary components of any constitution that could be considered "ecological" in nature. In particular, it argues that an ecological constitution is one that codifies the following key principles, at a minimum: the principle of sustainability; intergenerational equity and the public trust doctrine; environmental human rights; rights of nature; the precautionary principle and non-regression; and rights and obligations relating to a healthy climate. In the context of the global environmental crisis that characterises the current Anthropocene era, these principles are important tools for changing consciousness and driving pragmatic policy reforms around the world. Re-imagining constitutions along these lines could play a vital role in the collective project of building a sustainable future for humans, animals, ecosystems and the biosphere we all share.

This book will be of great interest to students and scholars of environmental law, ecological law, environmental constitutionalism, sustainability and rights of nature.

Lynda Collins is a Full Professor with the Centre for Environmental Law and Global Sustainability at the University of Ottawa, Canada.

Routledge Focus on Environment and Sustainability

For more information about this series, please visit: *www.routledge. com/Routledge-Focus-on-Environment-and-Sustainability/book-series/RFES*

The Ecological Constitution
Reframing Environmental Law

Lynda Collins

Routledge
Taylor & Francis Group

LONDON AND NEW YORK

First published 2021
by Routledge
2 Park Square, Milton Park, Abingdon, Oxon OX14 4RN

and by Routledge
605 Third Avenue, New York, NY 10158

Routledge is an imprint of the Taylor & Francis Group, an informa business

British Library Cataloguing-in-Publication Data
A catalogue record for this book is available from the British Library

Library of Congress Cataloging-in-Publication Data
Names: Collins, Lynda, author.
Title: The ecological constitution: reframing
environmental law/Lynda Collins.
Description: Milton Park, Abingdon, Oxon; New York,
NY: Routledge, 2021. | Series: Routledge focus on
environment and sustainability | Includes bibliographical
references and index.
Identifiers: LCCN 2021006832 (print) |
LCCN 2021006833 (ebook) | ISBN 9780367228729 (hardback) |
ISBN 9781032052113 (paperback) | ISBN 9780429277320 (ebook)
Subjects: LCSH: Environmental law. | Sustainable
development—Law and legislation. | Pollution—Law and
legislation. | Climatic changes—Law and legislation. |
Human rights. | Ecology.
Classification: LCC K3585.C6583 2021 (print) |
LCC K3585 (ebook) | DDC 344.04/6—dc23
LC record available at https://lccn.loc.gov/2021006832
LC ebook record available at https://lccn.loc.gov/2021006833

ISBN: 978-0-367-22872-9 (hbk)
ISBN: 978-1-032-05211-3 (pbk)
ISBN: 978-0-429-27732-0 (ebk)

Typeset in Times New Roman
by codeMantra

To my parents, who make the world a better place.

Contents

Preface

By Dr. David R. Boyd,
UN Special Rapporteur on human rights
and the environment

Earth is the only planet in the universe known to support life. The stable climate of the Holocene epoch enabled the emergence and evolution of human civilisation. Unfortunately, because of human activities, carbon dioxide concentrations in the atmosphere are at their highest level in millions of years; one million species are at risk of extinction; nine million people die prematurely every year from pollution; and there has been a surge of emerging infectious diseases of zoonotic origin, exemplified by the catastrophic COVID-19 pandemic. As the interlocking crises of climate disruption, biodiversity collapse, pervasive pollution and pandemics deepen, it is increasingly apparent that the fundamental legal rules governing human societies need to be rewritten. As world-leading scientists with the Intergovernmental Panel on Climate Change, Intergovernmental Science-Policy Platform on Biodiversity and Ecosystem Services and World Health Organization have concluded, humanity must make rapid, systemic and transformative changes in order to secure a sustainable future.

An essential element of this transformation involves imagining, enacting and implementing ecological constitutions at the national and global levels. Why focus on constitutions? These paramount laws, the supreme laws of all nations, set out the rules that all of society must abide by, including human rights and government responsibilities. Constitutions articulate who we are as a nation, and who we aspire to become. Our current constitutions are failing us. From the drafting of the American constitution in 1776 through to today, constitutions across the globe have been complicit in the great human conceit that we are somehow separate from, and even superior to, the rest of the natural world. In fact, *homo sapiens* share DNA with every other form of living being on the planet, meaning we are all related. It is a delusion to believe that our unique and unparalleled ingenuity will allow us to escape from the universal application of the laws of Nature. We govern ourselves as though the fundamental physical laws ruling the planet apply to the other 10 million or so species but don't apply to *homo sapiens*. Yet there are no loopholes in the laws of thermodynamics. Humanity cannot disrupt natural global cycles with impunity.

Therefore, we must import science into the very heart of our modern political and legal systems, the constitution. The concept of an ecological constitution may strike many as a novel idea, but it actually has deep roots in Indigenous cultures around the world. As Professor John Borrows has written, "The land's sentience is a fundamental principle of Anishinabek law", and it contributes to "a multiplicity of citizenship rights and responsibilities for Anishinabek people and the Earth".[1] Well before the dawn of the environmental era, in an article published in the journal *Ecology* in 1936, scientist W.P. Taylor called for the development of an ecological constitution, suggesting that the preamble include "a declaration of interdependence among plants, animals, and their environment".[2]

This engaging and insightful book offers a blueprint for rewriting the ground rules of civilisation. Professor Lynda Collins outlines the broad strokes and key elements of an ecological constitution, that is, a supreme law fit for purpose given the existential crisis facing humanity in the early 21st century. As Professor Collins eloquently articulates, an ecological constitution:

- recognises humanity's fundamental dependence on the natural world for our survival and well-being;
- replaces the anthropocentric perspective with an eco-centric viewpoint;
- clarifies that all human activities are subject to over-riding laws of Nature;
- acknowledges that all persons have environmental rights and responsibilities;
- imposes upon governments the responsibility for ensuring that the environmental rights of both persons and Nature are respected, protected and fulfilled; and
- identifies crucial guiding principles including polluter pays, precaution, the public trust, *in dubio pro natura*, and non-regression.

Today, the majority of the world's constitutions establish environmental rights and responsibilities but too many of these provisions do not go far enough, or have proven to be paper tigers. Ecuador's 2008 Constitution provides a stunning ray of hope. With its ground-breaking recognition of the rights of Pachamama (Mother Earth), revolutionary focus on living a good life in harmony with Nature and comprehensive array of environmental rights and responsibilities, it may well be the world's first ecological constitution. The proposed Global Pact for the Environment and the proposed Universal Declaration of the Rights of Mother Earth represent models for an ecological constitution at the international level.

Ecological constitutions highlight that Nature is not merely a commodity for humans to exploit but rather an extraordinary community to which we are blessed to belong. They acknowledge that the evolution of the Earth's life support systems is a miracle of the highest order, enabling us to call this beautiful blue-green planet our home. Humans, like all forms of life, require a healthy biosphere to survive, prosper and flourish. Ecological constitutions, by recognising scientific reality, offer one of humanity's last, best hopes for overcoming our self-destructive hubris and securing a sustainable future.

Notes

1 J. Borrows, *Canada's Indigenous Constitution* (Toronto: University of Toronto Press, 2010).
2 W.P. Taylor, "What Is Ecology and What Good Is It?" (1936) 17:3 *Ecology* 333–346 at 335.

Acknowledgements

I would like to express my heartfelt appreciation to David Boyd, Louis Kotzé and Carla Sbert (who introduced me to ecological law through her own brilliant work on the subject) for invaluable insights and comments on this project. I am equally indebted to Clémence Thabet and Loujain ElSahli for outstanding research assistance. Likewise, I am grateful to the University of Ottawa Faculty of Law, Research Office (under the outstanding leadership of Professor Penelope Simons) for generous financial support. Thanks also to Routledge and in particular to Annabelle Harris who championed the book proposal and to Matthew Shobbrook who kept me going during the difficult months of the COVID pandemic and, with the invaluable assistance of Karthikeyan S, saw the project through to completion. Most importantly, I am so grateful to my wonderful family who continually inspire, support and delight me: my parents, Donna Ouchterlony, Frank Collins, David Ouchterlony and Rachel Irskine; my honorary parents, Baidar and Anita Bakht; my siblings, Lisa Crossley, Julia Collins, Janet and Geordie Ouchterlony, Sacha Bakht and Heather Brady Bakht; my aunts, Laurie Buchfuhrer and Mary Collins; and my chosen family, Justine Bouquier (and Ollie), Natasha Bakht and Elaan Bakht. Thanks also to Sarah Rubenstein, Heather McLeod-Kilmurray, Graham Mayeda, Jamie Chai Yun Liew, Gabriel Dolo-Cooper, Meera Karunananthan and Nathalie Chalifour; I am lucky to have the best friends on Earth. Finally, I am grateful to my colleagues and students at the University of Ottawa's Center for Environmental Law and Global Sustainability; thank you for your guidance, friendship and encouragement.

1 Introduction

Constitutionalism in the age of ecological law

The application of constitutional thinking to our current ecological crisis raises several compelling questions: what would an ecological constitution look like? Put another way, how can states constitutionally ensure their ongoing survival on planet Earth? More provocatively, how relevant is a constitution that fails to make the attempt? This book makes a simple argument: domestic constitutions around the world should seek to protect the ecological foundation on which all societies stand. Thus far, our collective systems of environmental law and governance have failed to divert us from the path to catastrophe.[1] An ecological constitution could re-orient nation-states towards more viable development pathways; it would provide a lodestar for environmental law and could infuse all domestic laws with an ecological consciousness.

Although ecological sustainability requires international cooperation, and there is much work to be done to improve international environmental law (notably through the development of a global ecological constitution that complies with planetary boundaries),[2] this volume will focus on domestic constitutions as one tool for achieving planetary sustainability through the accretion of coordinated local action. The book proceeds in eight chapters. Chapter 1 introduces the concept of the ecological constitution, situating it at the confluence of ecological law and environmental constitutionalism. Chapter 2 advances an argument for ecological sustainability as a constitutional imperative and describes the growing body of existing constitutional provisions that already recognise this crucial overarching concept. Chapter 3 considers human rights in the ecological constitution, with a particular focus on the right to a healthy environment and Indigenous environmental rights.

Chapter 4 explores the constitutionalisation of intergenerational equity and the public trust doctrine, arguing that ecological constitutionalism requires a long-term perspective that enfranchises future generations of humans and other living beings. Chapter 5 introduces the precautionary principle and the associated principles of *in dubio pro natura* and non-regression, which have already been recognised in constitutional environmental law in some nations. Chapter 6 explores the most transformative (and rapidly expanding) area of ecological constitutionalism: rights of nature, or the idea that plants, animals, ecosystems and the Earth itself enjoy juridical personality and fundamental rights. Chapter 7 considers the emerging trend of "climate constitutionalism",[3] and Chapter 8 presents a brief conclusion, linking ecological constitutionalism with governance. As a whole, the volume maps out an "ecological transformation"[4] of domestic constitutions in order to align the highest forms of domestic law with the non-negotiable laws of nature. Such alignment is urgently needed in the Anthropocene era.

Welcome to the Anthropocene[5]

Much has been written about the unprecedented socio-ecological crisis that is currently unfolding around the globe; the grim evidence of our collective jeopardy will not be repeated here in any detail.[6] It suffices to observe that the present "Anthropocene" era is characterised by profound anthropogenic disruptions in the ecosphere.[7] Put simply, humans have now eroded natural systems on a global scale and to an extent that threatens the present and future well-being of people, plants, animals and ecosystems. We have crossed "planetary boundaries" that delineate the "safe operating space for humanity".[8] However, the news is not all bad; scientific, technical, economic and policy solutions abound.[9] Collectively, we have the resources and expertise to transition to more sustainable modes of living.

The crucial task now is to reimagine environmental law (and legal systems as a whole) in ways that will produce the necessary transformations. As Kotzé eloquently observes:

> The new epistemological space of the Anthropocene ... rejects an objectified, removed and simplified external nature that people are unable to understand or to care for, but able to exploit without limits. It invites instead a more enlightened view of human-nature relations that requires a deliberate effort to shift the parochial human-dominant exploitative focus of our regulatory institutions to a more inclusive ecological one.[10]

In other words, we need a new regulatory paradigm to remedy the failures of existing environmental laws and set a course for a sustainable future.

Re-visioning environmental law

Despite their many significant victories,[11] our existing environmental law regimes have thus far failed to prevent or reverse the eco-social crises of the Anthropocene. Indeed, environmental law has proven wholly inadequate when assessed against the crucial parameter of sustainability (i.e. the capacity of societies to survive and thrive over the coming decades and centuries).[12]

There are many reasons for this failure, including the problem of "agency capture", the underfunding or even outright rejection of environmental science, corporate hegemony and public apathy or overwhelm in the face of daunting environmental threats.[13] Moreover, the regulatory agencies tasked with developing and enforcing environmental law tend to be highly complex, isolated from each other and from ecological realities, inaccessible to the non-expert public and vulnerable to political and economic pressures that have no respect for fundamental ecological imperatives.[14] Meanwhile, courts have habitually deferred to governments' environmental decisions, even where such decisions are palpably unsustainable.[15]

Underlying the multiple factors contributing to the chronic underperformance of environmental law is a more elemental "failure to recognise the laws of nature and the fact that the Earth is finite".[16] Existing environmental laws are premised on a worldview that erroneously sees humans as separate from the natural "environment"[17] (the *other*), which is itself treated as though it had an infinite carrying capacity. Thus, the ecological inadequacy of environmental law is written into its DNA. Moreover, environmental law is embedded in unsustainable, "growth-insistent" economic systems that undermine its potential at every turn.[18] As a result, environmental law around the world is largely "anthropocentric, fragmented and ... politically weak as it competes with other, more powerful areas of law such as individualized property and corporate rights".[19]

Indeed, as Wood has shown, much environmental legislation is actually aimed at facilitating the exploitation of commodified natural resources, rather than preserving the stability and resilience of natural systems.[20] To summarise, "our system of laws does not protect the Earth from destruction because that is not its ultimate purpose, and, for this reason, a paradigm shift is needed".[21] One response to this urgent need to re-vision environmental law in more effective ways has been the invocation of constitutional rights and remedies.

The rise of environmental rights

In the decades since the 1972 *Stockholm Declaration* famously recognised the human right to a healthy environment, the majority of the world's states have chosen to include some form of environmental right and/or obligation in their constitutions.[22] United Nations Special Rapporteur on Human Rights and the Environment, David Boyd, reports that "more than 80 percent of States Members of the United Nations (156 out of 193) legally recognise the right to a safe, clean, healthy and sustainable environment".[23] At present, the domestic constitutions of at least 110 states explicitly protect the right to a healthy environment (variously described),[24] while 126 states have ratified regional treaties that include such a right, and 101 states have codified substantive environmental rights in national legislation.[25] A smaller group of states have evolved a constitutional right to environment through judicial interpretation of pre-existing rights, such as the right to life, health and/or dignity.[26]

As Boyd has written, "these constitutional developments appear to reflect a rapid evolution of human values, with environmental protection gaining the requisite moral importance to merit inclusion in written documents that express a society's most cherished and deeply held values".[27] More recently, this evolution has gone further, as a small but significant number of states and subnational jurisdictions have come to recognise the inherent rights of nature itself through constitutional provisions, legislation and case law.[28] This phenomenon coincides with the emergence of ecological law thinking around the world.

Introducing ecological law

The ecological law movement has recently emerged as an alternative to conventional environmental law, advancing a paradigm shift that "internalizes the natural living conditions of human existence and makes them the basis of all law, including constitutions, human rights, property rights, corporate rights and state sovereignty".[29] Variously formulated as "sustainability law"[30] "Earth jurisprudence",[31] "wild law"[32] and "green legal theory"[33] ecological law proposes a fundamental restructuring of human relationships with the Earth. As with many Indigenous legal systems around the world, ecological law flows from the basic recognition that "at a primary level, human society is a subset of the ecosphere".[34] Similar to the Andean Indigenous concepts loosely translated as *convivir bien* (or living/coexisting well together),[35] ecological law represents an alternative – rather than a reform – to existing systems.

The international foundations of ecological law are clearly visible in many provisions of the Earth Charter of the year 2000[36] and are even more explicit in the 2010 Universal Declaration on the Rights of Mother Earth.[37] The 2016 Oslo Manifesto for Ecological Law and Governance further develops its purpose, scope and content, declaring:

> To overcome the flaws of environmental law, mere reform is not enough. We do not need more laws, but different laws from which no area of the legal system is exempted. The ecological approach to law is based on ecocentrism, holism, and intra-/intergenerational and inter-species justice. From this perspective, or worldview, the law will recognise ecological interdependencies and no longer favour humans over nature and individual rights over collective responsibilities.[38]

The Siena Declaration of 2017 builds on the Oslo Manifesto, calling for a new comprehensive framework for law and governance that:

1 PROMOTES the entire Earth, the ecological whole, in decision-making;
2 VIEWS humans as a part of ecosystems and not separate from them;
3 RECOGNISES the level of specificity and contextuality needed in knowledge and practice to ensure the health of ecosystems;
4 PROMOTES ecological literacy and education that unites disciplines with a common ecological understanding and a new language, with a transdisciplinary and systematic approach, and strong ties between science and law;
5 RECOGNISES the limits to human understanding;
6 ADVANCES the precautionary principle;
7 ADVOCATES an Earth democracy philosophy, where everyone in our societies has a role to play as ecological citizens;
8 UNDERSTANDS the critical importance of voices and experiences from local and Indigenous communities that live in harmony with nature;

9 VIEWS that individuals, organisations, government entities and sovereign states are global agents of nature protection;

10 RECOGNISES the need to adjust notions of state sovereignty, where the whole shapes the parts and the parts shape the whole, while avoiding any part to undermine the whole;

11 UNDERSTANDS that common property and state sovereignty can coexist;

12 REDEFINES the commons as the entire Earth system, not simply the leftovers of state sovereignty;

13 RECOGNISES the need for new processes of decision-making, giving nature a voice at the table and addressing the failure of negotiation procedures to protect the foundations of life;

14 ADVANCES legal mechanisms that prioritise preserving ecosystem functionality in decision-making and give nongovernmental organisations and individuals the rights to represent nature;

15 ADVOCATES for the rights of nature and the further development of their scale, scope and practice;

16 IMPLEMENTS and EXPANDS the constitutional right to a healthy environment;

17 REQUIRES that actions in the short-term be constrained by the need to preserve the life-supporting properties of the Earth, its systems, the biosphere and its ecosystems in the long-term; and

18 ADVANCES social and economic development based on sound ecological principles.[39]

Elaborating on these basic principles in her ground-breaking work, *The Lens of Ecological Law*, Carla Sbert posits that any "ecological" legal order or instrument must exhibit at least three basic characteristics – ecocentrism, ecological primacy and ecological justice, defined as follows:

> Ecocentrism: Recognize and respect the value of all beings and the interconnectedness among them, equitably promoting the interests of human and nonhuman members of the Earth community.[40]

> Ecological Primacy: Ensure that social and economic behavior and systems are ecologically bound, respecting planetary boundaries.[41]

> Ecological justice: Ensure equitable access to the Earth's sustaining capacity for present and future generations of humans

and other beings, and avoid the inequitable allocation of environmental harms.[42]

Sbert's insightful elaboration of ecological law builds on foundational work by Garver, who views ecological law as a "complement to degrowth economics",[43] i.e. a means of constraining economic activity within ecological limits. Garver's "rule of ecological law" would be equitable, precautionary, adaptive, binding and based in the recognition that humanity is embedded in finite Earth systems.[44] Like Bosselmann's "principle of sustainability" (discussed in Chapter 2), Garver argues that "the rule of ecological law must permeate legal regimes", suggesting that constitutional codification may be necessary.[45] Moreover:

> Ecological law is firmly grounded in the science of how the Earth works and of complex systemic thresholds in the global ecosystem, and therefore combines legal principles with scientific laws of ecology as expressed, for example, in planetary boundaries. Yet, science alone cannot determine its elements.... Beyond science, ecological law derives from a fundamental normative choice to manage the human enterprise so as to offer up circumstances to which ecology, thermodynamics and the other sciences will apply in ways that preserve ecological integrity and keep the human-Earth relationship flourishing.[46]

Though the field continues to evolve and expand, ecological law is beginning to take shape, with clear implications for the ways in which we regulate the human-nature interface. While a detailed exposition of the content and implications of ecological law would merit its own lengthy volume,[47] a few concrete illustrations may be useful. An ecological legal order would regulate ecological realities rather than legal fictions. For example, ecological pollution regulation would include binding ambient standards (i.e. standards that put a hard cap on pollutant levels in air and water) to control cumulative emissions, rather than regulating specific "point sources" as if they existed in isolation.[48] Similarly, ecological assessments of specific projects would address all of their cumulative impacts on local and global ecosystems, including any increases in greenhouse gas emissions that might result from their construction. Ecological law also requires the *restoration* of ecosystems that are currently degraded or at risk.[49]

The ecological law paradigm also recognises the need to be cautious (or even sceptical) about our ability to predict the impacts of human activity on dynamic ecological systems. Both traditional Indigenous knowledge and modern ecology point to the immense complexity of natural systems and the intractable uncertainty that follows. As Maori leader Kristi Luke explains, "Our miniscule brain cannot perceive what is the might and sophistication of nature. We are never going to understand it all...".[50] Thus, rather than believing that we can successfully manage a forest, lake or fishery, this approach recognises that such systems are self-managing and the best thing we can do for them is to get out of the way.[51] While this is an impossible goal in many cases, a frank recognition of difficulties of prediction in ecology militates strongly in favour of precautionary regulation.

In particular, as Olivia Woolley has argued in her pivotal book, *Ecological Governance*, governments should implement a policy in favour of preserving ecological resilience and should assume that any stressors introduced by human activity tend to undermine such resilience.[52] Second, because natural systems function best when human impacts are minimised, ecological law requires a significant portion of territory to be preserved in protected areas (in a manner consistent with Indigenous rights), in which commercial-scale extractive activities are prohibited.[53]

In summary, ecological law has the potential to transform human behaviour by aligning legal systems with the ground-rules of life on Earth. If we accept that the laws of nature do indeed constrain all human endeavour, then it makes sense to recognise this reality in the highest form of human-made law within any state: the constitution.

Ecological constitutionalism in context

Before outlining the specific principles and provisions that should be incorporated into an ecological constitution, a few overarching considerations should be noted. First, since ecological constitutionalism is fundamentally oriented towards making meaningful change in the real world, eco-constitutional provisions must be enforceable rather than aspirational.[54] Thus, drafters should include ecological provisions in the actionable (i.e. self-executing) sections of their respective constitutions and judges should find such provisions to be justiciable. Second, to facilitate implementation, ecological constitutions should establish governmental authorities charged with advising the executive and legislative branches and enforcing constitutional environmental rights and duties in court. For example, the constitution of Brazil empowers the Ministerio Publico to prosecute violations of environmental laws (including the constitutional right to a healthy environment), and the Ministerio has made frequent and effective use of this power over the years.[55]

Third, as a complement to governmental implementation, ecological constitutions will need to include standing provisions that allow any member of the public or nongovernmental organisation to bring actions for enforcement. For example, Ecuador's famous 2008 constitution includes a provision declaring that "[a]ll persons, communities, peoples and nations can call upon public authorities to enforce the rights of nature"[56] and another that allows "any natural person or legal entity, human community or group" access to judicial and administrative bodies in order to guarantee the right to a healthy and ecologically balanced environment.[57]

Fourth, ecological constitutions should make specific provision for promoting access to justice and the expeditious resolution of constitutional environmental claims. Many Latin American nations have constitutional provisions establishing lower-cost, simplified legal procedures (e.g. the *amparo* and *tutela*) that "dramatically increase access to the judicial system in constitutional cases".[58] In India, public interest litigation procedures have similarly improved access to justice in constitutional matters, though major challenges remain.[59] In the Philippines, the Writ of Kalikasan (nature) provides an expedited process for cases involving an actual or threatened violation of the constitutional right to a balanced and healthful ecology involving "environmental damage of such magnitude as to prejudice the life, health or property of inhabitants of two or more cities or provinces".[60] These kinds of provisions could be replicated around the world.

Fifth, in federal states, ecological constitutionalism requires that courts recognise the broadest possible jurisdiction for each level of government to pursue ecological sustainability.[61] "Jurisdictional wrangling" cannot be allowed to impede crucial environmental protection initiatives such as greenhouse gas regulation.[62]

Finally, since the real world is ecologically connected on a global level, ecological constitutionalism inevitably requires international cooperation. In addition to the important efforts to optimise international environmental law and create a truly global environmental constitution,[63] developing nations will require international assistance to leap-frog unsustainable modes of development and have the opportunity to implement eco-constitutional approaches on the ground.

Bearing in mind these important contextual prerequisites, what is meant by "ecological constitutionalism"?[64] What would a constitution look like if it genuinely attempted to preserve a nation-state ecologically over time?[65] As Colombia's Constitutional Court has eloquently explained, "the Ecological Constitution ... is far from being a simple rhetorical [concept] insofar as it comprises a precise normative content composed of principles, fundamental rights and obligations ... of the State".[66] The remaining chapters of this book will elaborate on this idea by sketching out a kind of blueprint for how to build an ecological constitution.

Notes

1 See United Nations Environment Programme, *Global Environment Outlook GEO-6: Healthy Planet, Healthy People* (Cambridge: Cambridge University Press, 2019) [United Nations, *GEO-6*]; Jeremy Davies, *The Birth of the Anthropocene* (Oakland: University of California Press, 2016).

2 Louis J Kotzé, *Global Environmental Constitutionalism in the Anthropocene* (Oxford: Hart Publishing, 2016) [Kotzé, *Global Environmental Constitutionalism*]; Paulo Magalhães et al., eds, *The Safe Operating Space Treaty: A New Approach to Managing Our Use of the Earth System* (Cambridge: Cambridge Scholars, 2016).

3 Jordi Jaria-Manzano and Susana Borrás, eds, *Research Handbook on Climate Constitutionalism* (Cheltenham: Edward Elgar, 2019).

4 See Carla Sbert, *The Lens of Ecological Law: A Look at Mining* (Cheltenham: Edward Elgar, 2020) at 219 [Sbert, *Lens of Ecological Law*].

5 Alice Major, *Welcome to the Anthropocene* (Edmonton: University of Alberta Press, 2018).

6 See e.g. United Nations, *GEO-6*, *supra* note 1; Almut Arneth et al., *Climate Change and Land: An IPCC Special Report on Climate Change, Desertification, Land Degradation, Sustainable Land Management, Food Security, and Greenhouse Gas Fluxes in Terrestrial Ecosystems* (Geneva: IPCC, 2019).

7 See Davies, *supra* note 1; Colin N Waters et al., "The Anthropocene Is Functionally and Stratigraphically Distinct from the Holocene" (2016) 351:6269 Science 137.

8 Will Steffen, "The Planetary Boundaries Framework: Defining a Safe Operating Space for Humanity" in Paulo Magalhães et al., *supra* note 2, 23 at 24.

9 See e.g. T Altenburg and C Assman, eds, *Green Industrial Policy: Concept, Policies, Country Experiences* (Nairobi: United Nations Environment Programme, 2018); David R Boyd, *The Optimistic Environmentalist: Progressing towards a Greener Future* (Toronto: ECW Press,

2015) [Boyd, *Optimistic Environmentalist*]; David Miller, *Solved: How the World's Great Cities Are Fixing the Climate Crisis* (Toronto: University of Toronto Press, 2020).

10 Kotzé, *Global Environmental Constitutionalism, supra* note 2 at 30–31.

11 See generally Boyd, *Optimistic Environmentalist, supra* note 9.

12 See Klaus Bosselmann, *The Principle of Sustainability: Transforming Law and Governance*, 2nd ed. (London: Routledge, 2016) at 12 [Bosselmann, *Principle of Sustainability*]; Mary Christina Wood, *Nature's Trust: Environmental Law for a New Ecological Age* (Cambridge: Cambridge University Press, 2013).

13 Bosselmann, *Principle of Sustainability, supra* note 12; Wood, *supra* note 12. See also Penelope Simons and Audrey Macklin, *The Governance Gap: Extractive Industries, Human Rights, and the Home State Advantage* (New York: Routledge, 2014); David R Boyd, *Unnatural Law: Rethinking Canadian Environmental Law and Policy* (Vancouver: UBC Press, 2003) [Boyd, *Unnatural Law*].

14 Geoffrey Garver, *Ecological Law and the Planetary Crisis: A Legal Guide for Harmony on Earth* (London: Routledge, 2020) at 65–90 [Garver, *Planetary Crisis*]; Craig Collins, *Toxic Loopholes: Failures and Future Prospects for Environmental Law* (Cambridge: Cambridge University Press, 2010); Boyd, *Unnatural Law, supra* note 13.

15 See e.g. Jason MacLean and Chris Tollefson, "Climate-Proofing Judicial Review after Paris: Judicial Competence, Capacity, and Courage" (2018) 31:3 J Envtl L Prac 245 at 247–52; Lynda M Collins, "Judging the Anthropocene: Transformative Adjudication for the Anthropocene Epoch" in Louis Kotzé, ed., *Environmental Law and Governance for the Anthropocene* (Oxford: Hart Publishing, 2017) 309.

16 David R Boyd, "Sustainability Law: (R)Evolutionary Directions for the Future of Environmental Law" (2004) 14 J Envtl L Prac 357 at 365 [Boyd, "Sustainability Law"].

17 Ecological law thinkers generally prefer the notions of ecosystems, the Earth or Nature to that of "the environment", which suggests a separation between humans and nature that does not exist. However, we are currently in a transitional period in which the language of environmentalism is still used to refer to the ecological world and, like many others, this book will occasionally use the terms "environmental" and "ecological" interchangeably. See e.g. Klaus Bosselmann and Prue Taylor, *Ecological Approaches to Environmental Law* (Cheltenham: Edward Elgar, 2017).

18 Garver, *Planetary Crisis, supra* note 14 at 4.

19 Ecological Law and Governance Association (ELGA), "'Oslo Manifesto' for Ecological Law and Governance" (June 2016), online: *ELGA* <https://elgaworld.org/oslo-manifesto> at para 4 [ELGA, "Oslo Manifesto"].

20 Wood, *supra* note 12.

21 Nathalie Rühs and Aled Jones, "The Implementation of Earth Jurisprudence through Substantive Constitutional Rights of Nature" (2016) 8:2 Sustainability 174 at 175; see also Kirsten Anker et al., eds, *From Environmental to Ecological Law* (Abingdon: Routledge, 2020); Dayna Nadine Scott, "Confronting Chronic Pollution: A Socio-Legal Analysis of Risk and Precaution" (2008) 46:2 Osgoode Hall LJ 293.

22 See generally James R May and Erin Daly, *Global Environmental Constitutionalism* (Cambridge: Cambridge University Press, 2014); David R Boyd, *The Environmental Rights Revolution: A Global Study of Constitutions, Human Rights, and the Environment* (Vancouver: UBC Press, 2012) [Boyd, *Environmental Rights Revolution*]; Tim Hayward, *Constitutional Environmental Rights* (Oxford: Oxford University Press, 2004).

23 United Nations Special Rapporteur on the Issue of Human Rights Obligations Relating to the Enjoyment of a Safe, Clean, Healthy and Sustainable Environment, *Right to A Healthy Environment: Good Practices*, OHCHR, 43rd session, UN DOC A/HRC/43/53 (2020) at para 13.

24 *Ibid* at para 10 (noting that "Constitutional protection for [environmental] human rights is essential, because the constitution represents the highest and strongest law in a domestic legal system. Furthermore, the constitution plays an important cultural role, reflecting a society's values and aspirations".)

25 *Ibid* at paras 11–12.

26 See generally Donald K Anton and Dinah L Shelton, *Environmental Protection and Human Rights* (Cambridge: Cambridge University Press, 2011); Dinah Shelton, ed., *Human Rights and the Environment* (Cheltenham: Edward Elgar, 2011).

27 Boyd, *Environmental Rights Revolution, supra* note 22 at 76.

28 David R Boyd, *The Rights of Nature: A Legal Revolution That Could Save the World* (Toronto: ECW Press, 2017); Cameron La Follette and Chris Maser, *Sustainability and the Rights of Nature: An Introduction* (Boca Raton, FL: CRC Press, 2017).

29 ELGA, "Oslo Manifesto", *supra* note 19. See also Olivia Woolley, *Ecological Governance: Reappraising Law's Role in Protecting Ecosystem Functionality* (Cambridge: Cambridge University Press, 2014); see also Louis J Kotzé and Rakhyun E Kim, "Earth System Law: The Juridical Dimensions of Earth System Governance" (2019) 1 Earth Syst Gov 100003.

30 Boyd, "Sustainablity Law", *supra* note 16.

31 Peter D Burdon, *Earth Jurisprudence: Private Property and the Environment* (Oxon: Routledge, 2015); Thomas Berry, *The Great Work: Our Way into the Future* (New York: Bell Tower, 1999).

32 Cormac Cullinan, *Wild Law: A Manifesto for Earth Justice*, 2nd ed. (White River Junction, VT: Chelsea Green, 2011).

33 Michael M'Gonigle and Paula Ramsay, "Greening Environmental Law: From Sectoral Reform to Systemic Re-formation" (2004) 14 J Envtl L Prac 333.

34 John Borrows, "Living between Water and Rocks: First Nations, Environmental Planning and Democracy" (1997) 47:4 UTLJ 417.

35 Sbert, *Lens of Ecological Law, supra* note 4 at 170.

36 See "The Earth Charter 2000", as reprinted in Klaus Bosselmann and Ronald J Engel, eds, *The Earth Charter: A Framework for Global Governance* (Amsterdam: KIT, 2010) at 257–61.

37 See Evo M Ayma, *The Rights of Nature: The Case for a Universal Declaration of the Rights of Mother Earth* (Quito: Fundación Pachamama, 2011).

38 ELGA, "Oslo Manifesto", *supra* note 19.

39 ELGA, "Siena Declaration" (October 2017), online: *ELGA* <https://elgaworld.org/siena-declaration>.
40 Sbert, *Lens of Ecological Law, supra* note 4 at 78.
41 *Ibid* at 83.
42 *Ibid* at 92.
43 Geoffrey Garver, "The Rule of Ecological Law: The Legal Complement to Degrowth Economics" (2013) 5:1 Sustainability 316.
44 *Ibid.*
45 *Ibid* at 326. See also Garver, *Planetary Crisis, supra* note 18.
46 Garver, *Planetary Crisis, supra* note 18 at 95.
47 See e.g. Anker et al., *supra* note 21; Bosselmann and Taylor, *supra* note 17; Peter Burdon and Michelle Maloney, eds, *Wild Law – In Practice* (London: Routledge, 2014).
48 Lynda M Collins, "Security of the Person, Peace of Mind: A Precautionary Approach to Environmental Uncertainty" (2013) 4:1 J Hum Rts Envtl 79.
49 See e.g. Emilie Boulot, "Restoring Land, Restoring Law: Theorizing Ecological Law with Ecological Restoration" in Kirsten Anker et al., *supra* note 21.
50 Quoted in Craig M Kauffman, "Managing People for the Benefit of the Land: Practising Earth Jurisprudence in Te Urewera, New Zealand" (2020) 27:3 ISLE 578 at 588.
51 Cullinan, *supra* note 32.
52 *Ibid* at 27–39.
53 See generally Edward O Wilson, *Half-Earth: Our Planet's Fight for Life* (New York: Liveright, 2016). In creating such protected areas, states must be careful to respect, protect and fulfil Indigenous rights. See Marcus Colchester, "Indigenous Peoples and Protected Areas: Rights, Principles and Practice" 7:1 Nomadic Peoples 33.
54 See Boyd, *Environmental Rights Revolution, supra* note 22 at 71–77.
55 *Ibid* at 131–3.
56 *Constitution of 2008 of the Republic of Ecuador* (20 October 2008) at article 71.
57 *Ibid* at article 397.
58 Boyd, *Environmental Rights Revolution, supra* note 22 at 69.
59 James Fowkes, "How to Open the Doors of the Court: Lessons on Access to Justice from Indian PIL" (2011) 27:3 S Afr J Hum Rts 434.
60 See Hilario G Davide Jr, "The Environment as Life Sources and the Writ of Kalikasan in the Philippines" (2012) 29:2 Pace Envtl L Rev 592 at 597.
61 See e.g. Dayna Scott, "Federalism, the Environment and the Charter in Canada" in *The Law Society of Upper Canada, Special Lectures 2017: Canada at 150: The Charter and the Constitution* (Toronto, 2018) 188 at 188–201.
62 Nathalie J Chalifour, "Jurisdictional Wrangling over Climate Policy in the Canadian Federation: Key Issues in the Provincial Constitutional Challenges to Parliament's Greenhouse Gas Pollution Pricing Act" (2019) 50:2 Ottawa L Rev 197.
63 See e.g. Kotzé, *Global Environmental Constitutionalism, supra* note 2.

64 See Klaus Boselmman, "Eco-Constitutionalism: A New Area of Legal Research and Advocacy" (Address on International Developments delivered at Australia's Third Wild Law Conference, 16 September 2011)
65 See e.g. Klaus Bosselmann, *Im Namen der Natur: Der Weg zum ökologischen Rechtsstaat* (Munich: Scherz, 1992).
66 Constitutional Court of Columbia, 10 November 2016, *Center for Social Justice Studies et al v Presidency of the Republic et al*, Judgment T-622/16 at para 5.4. See also Oscar Darío Amaya Navas, *La Constitución Ecológica de Colombia*, 3rd ed. (Bogotá: Universidad Externado de Colombia).

References

Altenburg, Tilman & Claudia Assman, eds, *Green Industrial Policy: Concept, Policies, Country Experiences* (Nairobi: United Nations Environment Programme, 2018).
Anker, Kirsten et al., eds, *From Environmental to Ecological Law* (London: Routledge, 2020).
Anton, Donald K & Dinah L Shelton, *Environmental Protection and Human Rights* (Cambridge: Cambridge University Press, 2011).
Arnet, Almut et al., *Climate Change and Land: An IPCC Special Report on Climate Change, Desertification, Land Degradation, Sustainable Land Management, Food Security, and Greenhouse Gas Fluxes in Terrestrial Ecosystems* (Geneva: IPCC, 2019).
Ayma, Evo M, *The Rights of Nature: The Case for a Universal Declaration of the Rights of Mother Earth* (Quito: Fundación Pachamama, 2011).
Berry, Thomas, *The Great Work: Our Way into the Future* (New York: Bell Tower, 1999).
Borrows, John, "Living between Water and Rocks: First Nations, Environmental Planning and Democracy" (1997) 47:4 UTLJ 417.
Boselmman, Klaus, "Eco-Constitutionalism: A New Area of Legal Research and Advocacy" (Address on International Developments delivered at Australia's Third Wild Law Conference, 16 September 2011).
Bosselmann, Klaus, *Im Namen der Natur: Der Weg zum ökologischen Rechtsstaat* (Munich: Scherz, 1992).
Bosselmann, Klaus, *The Principle of Sustainability: Transforming Law and Governance*, 2nd ed. (London: Routledge, 2016).
Bosselmann, Klaus & Ronald J Engel, eds, *The Earth Charter: A Framework for Global Governance* (Amsterdam: KIT, 2010).
Bosselmann, Klaus & Prue Taylor, *Ecological Approaches to Environmental Law* (Cheltenham: Edward Elgar, 2017).
Boyd, David R, *The Environmental Rights Revolution: A Global Study of Constitutions, Human Rights, and the Environment* (Vancouver: UBC Press, 2012).
Boyd, David R, *The Optimistic Environmentalist: Progressing Towards a Greener Future* (Toronto: ECW Press, 2015).

Boyd, David R, *The Rights of Nature: A Legal Revolution That Could Save the World* (Toronto: ECW Press, 2017).

Boyd, David R, "Sustainability Law: (R)Evolutionary Directions for the Future of Environmental Law" (2004) 14 J Envtl L Prac 357.

Boyd, David R, *Unnatural Law: Rethinking Canadian Environmental Law and Policy* (Vancouver: UBC Press, 2003).

Boulot, Emille, "Restoring Land, Restoring Law: Theorizing Ecological Law with Ecological Restoration" in Kirsten Anker et al., eds, *From Environmental to Ecological Law* (London: Routledge, 2020) 76.

Burdon, Peter & Michelle Maloney, eds, *Wild Law – In Practice* (London: Routledge, 2014).

Burdon, Peter D, *Earth Jurisprudence: Private Property and the Environment* (Oxon: Routledge, 2015).

Center for Social Justice Studies et al v Presidency of the Republic et al [2016], Constitutional Court of Colombia 622/16.

Chalifour, Nathalie J, "Jurisdictional Wrangling over Climate Policy in the Canadian Federation: Key Issues in the Provincial Constitutional Challenges to Parliament's Greenhouse Gas Pollution Pricing Act" (2019) 50:2 Ottawa L Rev 197.

Colchester, Marcus, "Indigenous Peoples and Protected Areas: Rights, Principles and Practice" 7:1 Nomadic Peoples 33.

Collins, Craig, *Toxic Loopholes: Failures and Future Prospects for Environmental Law* (Cambridge: Cambridge University Press, 2010).

Collins, Lynda M, "Judging the Anthropocene: Transformative Adjudication for the Anthropocene Epoch" in Louis Kotzé, ed., *Environmental Law and Governance for the Anthropocene* (Oxford: Hart Publishing, 2017) 309.

Collins, Lynda M, "Security of the Person, Peace of Mind: A Precautionary Approach to Environmental Uncertainty" (2013) 4:1 J Hum Rts Envtl 79.

Constitution of 2008 of the Republic of Ecuador (20 October 2008).

Cullinan, Cormac, *Wild Law: A Manifesto for Earth Justice*, 2nd ed. (White River Junction, VT: Chelsea Green, 2011).

Davide Jr, Hilario G, "The Environment as Life Sources and the Writ of Kalikasan in the Philippines" (2012) 29:2 Pace Envtl L Rev 592.

Davies, Jeremy, *The Birth of the Anthropocene* (Oakland: University of California Press, 2016).

Ecological Law and Governance Association (ELGA), "'Oslo Manifesto' for Ecological Law and Governance" (June 2016), online: *ELGA* <https://elgaworld.org/oslo-manifesto>.

Ecological Law and Governance Association, "Siena Declaration" (October 2017), online: *ELGA* <https://elgaworld.org/siena-declaration>.

Fowkes, James, "How to Open the Doors of the Court: Lessons on Access to Justice from Indian PIL" (2011) 27:3 S Afr J Hum Rts 434.

Garver, Geoffrey, *Ecological Law and the Planetary Crisis: A Legal Guide for Harmony on Earth* (London: Routledge, 2020).

Garver, Geoffrey, "The Rule of Ecological Law: The Legal Complement to Degrowth Economics" (2013) 5:1 Sustainability 316.

Hayward, Tim, *Constitutional Environmental Rights* (Oxford: Oxford University Press, 2004).

Jaria-Manzano, Jordi & Susana Borrás, eds, *Research Handbook on Climate Constitutionalism* (Cheltenham: Edward Elgar, 2019).

Kauffman, Craig M, "Managing People for the Benefit of the Land: Practising Earth Jurisprudence in Te Urewera, New Zealand" (2020) 27:3 ISLE 578.

Kotzé, Louis J, *Global Environmental Constitutionalism in the Anthropocene* (Oxford: Hart Publishing, 2016).

Kotzé, Louis J & Rakhyun E Kim, "Earth System Law: The Juridical Dimensions of Earth System Governance" (2019) 1 Earth Syst Gov 100003.

LaFollette, Cameron & Chris Maser, *Sustainability and the Rights of Nature: An Introduction* (Boca Raton, FL: CRC Press, 2017).

MacLean, Jason & Chris Tollefson, "Climate-Proofing Judicial Review after Paris: Judicial Competence, Capacity, and Courage" (2018) 31:3 J Envtl L Prac 245.

Major, Alice, *Welcome to the Anthropocene* (Edmonton: University of Alberta Press, 2018).

Magalhães, Paulo et al., eds, *The Safe Operating Space Treaty: A New Approach to Managing Our Use of the Earth System* (Cambridge: Cambridge Scholars, 2016).

May, James R & Erin Daly, *Global Environmental Constitutionalism* (Cambridge: Cambridge University Press, 2014).

M'Gonigle, Michael & Paula Ramsay, "Greening Environmental Law: From Sectoral Reform to Systemic Re-formation" (2004) 14 J Envtl L Prac 333.

Miller, David, *Solved: How the World's Great Cities Are Fixing the Climate Crisis* (Toronto: University of Toronto Press, 2020).

Report of the Special Rapporteur on the Issue of Human Rights Obligations Relating to the Enjoyment of a Safe, Clean, Healthy and Sustainable Environment: Right to a Healthy Environment: Good Practices, OHCHR, 43rd Session, UN Doc A/HRC/43/53 (2020).

Rühs, Nathalie & Aled Jones, "The Implementation of Earth Jurisprudence through Substantive Constitutional Rights of Nature" (2016) 8:2 Sustainability 174.

Sbert, Carla, *The Lens of Ecological Law: A Look at Mining* (Cheltenham: Edward Elgar, 2020).

Scott, Dayna, "Federalism, the Environment and the Charter in Canada" in *The Law Society of Upper Canada, Special Lectures 2017: Canada at 150: The Charter and the Constitution* (Toronto: Irwin Law, 2017) 188.

Scott, Dayna N, "Confronting Chronic Pollution: A Socio-Legal Analysis of Risk and Precaution" (2008) 46:2 Osgoode Hall LJ 293.

Shelton, Dinah, *Human Rights and the Environment* (Cheltenham: Edward Elgar, 2011).

Simons, Penelope & Audrey Macklin, *The Governance Gap: Extractive Industries, Human Rights, and the Home State Advantage* (New York: Routledge, 2014).

Steffen, Will, "The Planetary Boundaries Framework: Defining a Safe Operating Space for Humanity" in Paulo Magalhães et al., eds, *The Safe Operating Space Treaty: A New Approach to Managing Our Use of the Earth System* (Cambridge: Cambridge Scholars, 2016) 23.

United Nations Environment Program, *Global Environment Outlook GEO-6: Healthy Planet, Healthy People* (Cambridge: Cambridge University Press, 2019).

Waters, Colin N et al., "The Anthropocene Is Functionally and Stratigraphically Distinct from the Holocene" (2016) 351:6269 Science 137.

Wilson, Edward O, *Half-Earth: Our Planet's Fight for Life* (New York: Liveright, 2016).

Wood, Mary C, *Nature's Trust: Environmental Law for a New Ecological Age* (Cambridge: Cambridge University Press, 2013).

Woolley, Olivia, *Ecological Governance: Reappraising Law's Role in Protecting Ecosystem Functionality* (Cambridge: Cambridge University Press, 2014).

2 The constitutional imperative of ecological sustainability

This chapter considers the central place of sustainability in ecological constitutionalism. Ecological sustainability can be defined as the long-term viability or well-being of ecological systems, including human communities.[1] Understood in this way, sustainability is the fundamental overarching principle that frames all other legal constructs in an ecological constitution. The history, scope and status of the principle of ecological sustainability have been authoritatively explicated in a voluminous and important body of work by Bosselmann, who describes the principle of sustainability "as the duty to protect and restore the integrity of the Earth's ecological systems".[2]

Ecological sustainability is a complex and contested concept.[3] It is much more specific than the idea of "sustainable development", which "eschews the language of both rights and responsibility ... and is highly ambiguous as a policy framework".[4] Though it extends well beyond the anthropocentric perspective, ecological sustainability is now viewed as a "substantive element" of the human right to a healthy environment,[5] encompassing the survival of nonhuman living beings and the viability of the ecosphere for future generations of humans and nonhumans alike.[6] It is the animating concept in Boyd's vision for "sustainability law", a system of law that would be "firmly rooted in science and the laws of nature, beginning with ... explicit recognition of the biophysical limits of the planet Earth".[7]

For proponents of ecological sustainability, a central problem is that of institutionalising and implementing it through legal mechanisms.[8] While there are myriad legal tools that could forward the project of ecological sustainability – everything from carbon taxes to endangered species legislation – one potentially transformative approach proposed by Bosselmann is the recognition of ecological sustainability as a fundamental legal principle.[9] At the international level, this would involve the enactment of a binding convention codifying obligations with respect to sustainability,[10] while at the domestic level it would almost certainly require constitutional recognition.[11]

Sustainability is well suited to constitutionalisation. Bosselmann has argued persuasively that "[ecological] sustainability has the historical, conceptual and ethical quality typical for a fundamental principle of law" and should "infor[m] the entire legal system, not just environmental laws...".[12] It is broad enough to function as an overarching principle guiding all aspects of a legal system, yet specific enough to provide meaningful guidance in the formulation of particular policies. The principle of ecological sustainability would reorient legal systems to recognise the primacy of ecosystems (and Earth systems) in all policymaking, starting with constitutions.[13]

The ecological purpose of constitutions

There can be little doubt that the ecological awakening necessary to save humanity from itself must reach far beyond legal systems. Profound shifts in thinking and practice must occur across all fields of social endeavour, including agriculture, architecture, housing, transportation, education, religion, philosophy, cultural production and politics.[14] Perhaps most crucially, no legal system can achieve ecological sustainability in the context of unsustainable economic patterns of production and consumption.[15]

Critics have questioned the adequacy, efficacy and even the legitimacy of constitutionalism as an approach to ecological sustainability,[16] yet leading scholars and advocates for ecological sustainability around the world continue to advocate for constitutionalisation.[17] Why? Perhaps most importantly, foundational work by Boyd and others has demonstrated convincingly that constitutional approaches to sustainability – in particular substantive environmental rights – have the potential to meaningfully improve states' environmental performance.[18] If this were the only support for ecological constitutionalism, it would be enough. However, the case for constitutionalising ecological principles goes beyond this important empirical basis, engaging the multiple roles and meanings of constitutions in the journey towards sustainability.

As a starting point, "[a]lthough the role of law in achieving sustainability is limited, it is important because only through law can we actually *coerce* ourselves".[19] Within the hierarchy of law, it makes sense to constitutionally enshrine any crucial public interest

since constitutions are supreme, overriding any contradictory legislation, constraining government conduct and thus guaranteeing
consistency over time. As one court put it, "[a] statute defines present rights and obligations. It is easily enacted and as easily repealed.
A constitution, by contrast, is drafted with an eye to the future.
Its function is to provide a continuing framework".[20] Given that
ecological sustainability is, by definition, a long-term project,[21] it
makes sense to codify it in the state's most enduring legal construct.

Constitutions represent a historic moment when society reaches
for the best of itself and attempts to protect its core values from the
political vacillations of successive governments. This is a particularly salient factor in the area of environmental protection, since
governments elected for a handful of years are wont to prioritise
short-term economic or political gains over long-term ecological
(and economic) sustainability.[22] Constitutions are also the only legal instruments that frame and permeate all areas of domestic law
and thus have the potential to move "environmental law" from the
margins into the very fabric of legal systems (including corporate,
financial and property law).[23]

Moreover, "[t]here is also a vital normative role for constitutions,
which express the deepest, most cherished values of a society".[24]
Constitutions both reflect and raise public consciousness and thus
hold the potential to create more ecological states and citizens,
since "[o]ur ideas about the nonhuman world themselves become
ecological actors, shaping our ethics and therefore our behaviors
towards the nonhuman world".[25] A constitutional "rule of law for
nature ... provides the means to dictate the content of laws; and
it establishes moral and ethical obligations with respect to the environment and a justificatory basis for, and authority to require,
proper performance of these obligations".[26]

Constitutions also open up a dialogic space for scholars and
advocates to re-vision eco-social and political systems that are re-
sponsive to the challenges of the Anthropocene:

> The constitution is ... a social construct, in which norms and
> practices are built and modified according to decisions of in-
> stitutional actors, but also through the legal culture, where
> academics can envisage new approaches and encourage new
> strategies. Considering the challenges that the Anthropocene
> presents regarding sustainability and justice, it seems neces-
> sary to work on the construction of fundamental constitutional
> ideas which can inspire [solutions].[27]

Even for pure constitutionalists who may have little interest in sustainability per se, the case for ecologising constitutions is inescapable, since a constitution cannot fulfil its primary role – to build and preserve a nation – in the absence of ecological sustainability. If the "the raison d'être of the modern state is to promote the interests of its citizens",[28] then an ecologically literate state must, of necessity, protect the natural systems in which every society is embedded.

This realisation has led to the phenomenon of "global environmental constitutionalism", defined by James May and Erin Daly as "the recognition that the environment is a proper subject for protection in constitutional texts and for vindication by constitutional courts worldwide".[29] Situating global environmental constitutionalism within the epistemic framework of the Anthropocene, Kotzé defines the concept as "both an analytical (or intellectual) perspective and a normative attempt ... to find traces of and to apply constitutionalism in global environmental law and governance".[30] Bosselmann, in turn, defines eco-constitutionalism as "...the adherence of any form of government to fundamental ecological principles" and concludes that "[t]he principle of [ecological] sustainability must be ... constitutionalized, so that the prevailing model will be the 'eco-constitutional' state".[31]

Conceding that the difference between "environmental" and "ecological" is often merely semantic, this book nonetheless favours the language of ecological law as a way to signal a radical departure from previous approaches that have treated the nonhuman natural world as an "environment" outside of and subject to human beings. Like scholars of environmental constitutionalism, I will advance a vision for ecological constitutionalism that goes beyond a description of practice, to embrace a normative dimension. For our purposes, ecological constitutionalism can be defined as "the study, practice and normative/ethical imperative of constitutionalising ecological principles to the extent necessary to ensure the long-term sustainability of the ecological systems upon which the enacting nation depends (including the ecosphere as a whole)".

However one chooses to define the concept, ecological constitutionalism has deep roots. In fact, "[t]he Earth-centred paradigm [is] guided by the oldest jurisprudential traditions of humankind".[32] Eco-centric or holistic legal approaches to the human–Earth relationship have been developed and nurtured globally by diverse Indigenous legal orders and are now being revitalised by Indigenous and non-Indigenous advocates and decision-makers around the world.

Sustainability provisions in existing constitutions

Given the evidence of ongoing environmental decline around the world, it seems clear that humanity needs to find a way to constrain its behaviour within ecological limits in order to achieve sustainability.

> [C]onstitutionalism happens to be rather familiar with imposing limitations and creating constraints. It might thus very well be that constitutionalism could be employed ... to [endow] sustainability with the higher order and supreme status of constitutional principles, values, norms, and standards.[33]

As with other fundamental concepts such as the rule of law, justice, equality and the like, constitutional recognition of ecological sustainability could potentially inform and animate the more specific and detailed provisions of a constitution, shaping legal culture and influencing judicial interpretation.[34] Recognizing its potential as a legal lodestar, a number of countries have attempted to constitutionalise sustainability or related concepts to some degree.

Boyd reports that as many as 140 national constitutions include some form of government obligation or responsibility to protect the environment, of which 82 are legally enforceable.[35] Some such provisions may reflect the principle of sustainability without actually using the term. For example, Korea's constitution provides that "The State shall adopt measures to protect the environment, *giving it preference over production*, preserve and promote the natural environment and prevent environmental pollution...".[36] The Ukraine's 1996 constitution makes "ensuring environmental safety [and] maintaining ecological balance ... a duty of the state" and Afghanistan's 2004 constitution provides that "[t]he state shall be obligated to adopt necessary measures to protect and improve forests as well as the living environment".[37] Similarly, Norway's environmental rights provision states that

> [e]very person has a right to an environment that is conducive to health and ... whose productivity and diversity are maintained. Natural resources shall be managed on the basis of comprehensive long-term considerations which will safeguard this right for future generations as well".[38]

In contrast, some constitutions specifically include the term "sustainable development" but emphasise natural resource exploitation rather than conservation. For example, the Constitution of Albania provides that the state "aims to supplement private initiative and responsibility with: Rational exploitation of forests, waters, pastures and other natural resources on the basis of the principle of sustainable development".[39] Applying Sbert's "lens of ecological law",[40] one can see that this provision does not meet the criteria of ecocentrism, ecological primacy or ecological justice. Similarly, Algeria's draft 2020 constitution (which has now been approved via referendum)[41] specifically prioritises economic growth, providing that "Citizens shall have the right to a healthy environment within a framework of sustainable growth".[42] Arguably, this represents a weakening of Algeria's previous environmental right provision, which stated simply that "Citizens shall have the right to a healthy environment".[43]

In other constitutions, the mention of sustainable development is embedded in a context that suggests a stronger form of ecological protection. In the Constitution of the Seychelles, for example, sustainable development is set out as a state obligation in the context of the right to a healthy environment, as follows:

> The State recognises the right of every person to live in and enjoy a clean, healthy and ecologically balanced environment and with a view to ensuring the effective realization of this right the State undertakes-
>
> a   to take measures to promote the protection, preservation and improvement of the environment
> b   to ensure a sustainable socio-economic development of Seychelles by a judicious use and management of the resources of Seychelles;
> c   to promote public awareness of the need to protect, preserve and improve the environment.[44]

Similarly, South Africa's constitutional right to a healthy environment includes the right

> to have the environment protected, for the benefit of present and future generations, through reasonable legislative and other measures that – i.prevent ... ecological degradation; ii.promote conservation; and iii.secure ecologically sustainable development and use of natural resources while promoting justifiable economic and social development.[45]

Anél Du Plessis explains that this provision imposes on the South African government "a weighty duty of trusteeship. The entire

government has the constitutional ... duty to protect natural resources, so that they will, among other things, be available to future
generations", i.e. a duty to achieve ecological sustainability.[46]

The constitutions of Ecuador and Bolivia take a unique approach
to sustainability, guided by the Indigenous idea of *buen vivir* (or *vivir
bien*) – a loose translation of the concepts of *sumak kawsay* in Quec-
hua or *suma qamaña* in the Aymara language.[47] Sbert explains that
the actual meaning of these terms, and related concepts from other
Andean Indigenous peoples, is "closer to *'vivir bien juntos/convivir
bien'* (live/co-exist well together) and reflects relations among humans as well as between humans and nature".[48] *Vivir bien* includes
"bio-ethics or respect for all life and the rights of (and stewardship
towards) non-human nature".[49] While Ecuador is most famous for
its robust and detailed constitutional recognition of the rights of
Pachamama or Mother Earth, it also specifically recognises the
goal of *vivir bien* in multiple provisions, including in its Preamble.[50]
Article 8 of the Bolivian Constitution of 2009 similarly identifies
vivir bien (*suma qamaña*) as "one of the ethical, moral principles of
the plural society".[51]

Like many of the sustainability provisions discussed above, the
constitutional recognition of *buen vivir* by Ecuador and Bolivia
may appear to be aspirational rather than justiciable. However, the
Constitutional Court of Ecuador has held that *buen vivir* and rights
of nature are central to the constitution and affect all other rights –
including property rights – thus justifying government interference
with unsustainable resource use.[52] Thus, it appears that these kinds
of provisions can influence the outcomes of litigation, at least in
some legal cultures. Nevertheless, May and Daly observe that for
the most part, "trends in ... 'sustainability constitutionalism' are
dichotomous. While the constitutions of nations now regularly incorporate sustainability, jurists and advocates have been slow to
promote it as a proper legal outcome instead of merely a silent guiding principle".[53]

Legal tools for incorporating ecological sustainability into constitutions

Constitutions can be ecologised through explicit amendment, judicial interpretation or some combination of the two. From the
perspective of environmental democracy, explicit amendment is
preferable, since it opens up a space for dialogue and delibera-
tion and increases the legitimacy of the outcomes. In the context

of the substantive right to a healthy environment, explicit textual recognition represents best practice,[54] and this likely holds true for the other kinds of ecological provisions discussed in this book. Certainly, the wholesale transformation of a constitution, such as occurred in post-apartheid South Africa or in Ecuador in 2008, demands an open public process resulting in explicit revisions to the constitutional text. However, the politics and procedure of constitutional amendment vary widely among nations, and, in some jurisdictions, it may be difficult or even impossible to achieve in the near term.[55]

In the absence of explicit amendment, ecological principles may still find their way into constitutions through judicial interpretation. In the context of our ongoing ecological crisis, many judges see the logic in measuring the legitimacy of state action by the extent to which it comports with non-derogable ecological laws. The Supreme Court of the Philippines eloquently captured this idea in its celebrated decision in *Minors Oposa*, an early case concerning the environmental rights of future generations:

> While the right to a balanced and healthful ecology is to be found under the Declaration of Principles and State Policies and not under the Bill of Rights, it does not follow that it is less important than any of the civil and political rights enumerated in the latter. Such a right belongs to a different category of rights altogether for it concerns nothing less than self-preservation and self-perpetuation[,] the advancement of which may even be said to predate all governments and constitutions. As a matter of fact, these basic rights need not even be written in the Constitution for they are assumed to exist from the inception of humankind.[56]

A United States District Court cited *Oposa* when denying the motion to dismiss the famous *Juliana* youth climate lawsuit,[57] holding that a stable climate might be an "unenumerated fundamental right" under the American constitution. The judge in this instance recognised that "a stable climate system is quite literally the foundation 'of society, without which there would be neither civilization nor progress'".[58] Although *Juliana* itself has floundered in later stages of litigation, the logic of these decisions seems inescapable. The principle of ecological sustainability is so fundamental as to be both implicit and obvious – a basic, underlying tenet that supports every other provision in a written constitution.[59]

There is growing precedent for the judicial recognition of ecological entitlements even in constitutions that lack explicit ecological language. For decades, courts in countries such as India, Pakistan, Sri Lanka and Nigeria (among others) have held that their respective constitutions' protection for the right to life encompasses the human right to adequate environmental conditions to permit a life of dignity.[60] Courts in India, Bangladesh and Colombia have also bridged the gap between anthropocentric and eco-centric environmental rights, recognising rights for rivers, animals and ecosystems (as elaborated in Chapter 5 – Rights of Nature).

In a particularly important development, Canadian, New Zealand, Colombian and Indian courts have broken new ground by recognising and implementing Indigenous legal and cultural principles relevant to sustainability.[61] Although Indigenous groups cannot be essentialised as inherently ecological actors,[62] courts should be willing to learn from Indigenous legal orders that successfully maintained respectful relations with nature for centuries or millennia before the advent of industrial capitalism and colonisation.[63] Recognising and effectuating Indigenous legal approaches to environmental protection (or "Indigenous environmental self-determination"[64]) could advance both ecological sustainability and reconciliation between Indigenous peoples and settlers.

Whatever method is chosen, the eco-social crises of the Anthropocene highlight the constitutional imperative of ecological sustainability. To serve their citizens, and preserve their own survival, states will need to find ways to constitutionalise ecological sustainability. As a starting point, Chapter 3 argues that all states should expand their existing conceptions of human rights to include the right to a "safe, clean, healthy and sustainable environment".[65]

Notes

1 See Klaus Bosselmann, *The Principle of Sustainability: Transforming Law and Governance*, 2nd ed. (London: Routledge, 2016) at 5 ("[S]ustainability means maintenance of the integrity of the Earth's ecological systems"); Cameron La Follette and Chris Maser, *Sustainability and the Rights of Nature: An Introduction* (Boca Raton, FL: CRC Press, 2017) at 99 ("Sustainability is flexible but maintains Nature's integrity").

2 Bosselmann, *The Principle of Sustainability*, *supra* note 1 at 53.

3 See e.g. Rebecca M Bratspies, "Sustainability: Can Law Meet the Challenge?" (2011) 34:2 Suffolk Transnat'l L Rev 283.

4 Lynda M Collins, "Revisiting the Doctrine of Intergenerational Equity in Global Environmental Governance" (2007) 30:1 Dal LJ 79 at 87; see

also Sam Adelman "The Sustainable Development Goals, Anthropocentrism and Neoliberalism" in Duncan French and Louis J Kotzé, eds, *Sustainable Development Goals: Law, Theory and Implementation* (Northampton, MA: Edward Elgar, 2018) 15.

5 See e.g. David R Boyd, *Report of the Special Rapporteur on the Issue of Human Rights Obligations Relating to the Enjoyment of a Safe, Clean, Healthy and Sustainable Environment*, OHCHR, 75th session, UN DOC A/75/161 (2020).

6 Bosselmann, *Principle of Sustainability, supra* note 1 at 118–23.

7 David R Boyd, "Sustainability Law: (R)Evolutionary Directions for the Future of Environmental Law" (2004) 14 J Envtl L Prac 357 at 367.

8 See e.g. Bratspies, *supra* note 3; Rakhyun E Kim and Klaus Bosselmann, "Operationalizing Sustainable Development: Ecological Integrity as a Grundnorm of International Law" (2015) 24:2 RECIEL 194.

9 Bosselmann, *Principle of Sustainability, supra* note 1.

10 One model would be to codify the existing, nonbinding *Earth Charter* into a binding international treaty; see Bosselmann, *Principle of Sustainability, supra* note 1 at 206–8.

11 See e.g. Lynda Collins, "The Unwritten Constitutional Principle of Ecological Sustainability: A Solution to the Pipelines Puzzle?" (2019) 70 UNBLJ 30; Bosselmann, *Principle of Sustainability, supra* note 1 at 158–9.

12 Bosselmann, *Principle of Sustainability, supra* note 1 at 4; Olivia Woolley, *Ecological Governance: Reappraising Law's Role in Protecting Ecosystem Functionality* (Cambridge: Cambridge University Press, 2014) at 96–98.

13 Bosselmann, *Principle of Sustainability, supra* note 1 at 166.

14 See e.g. Daniel Butt, "Law, Governance, and the Ecological Ethos" in Stephen M Gardiner and Allen Thompson, eds, *The Oxford Handbook of Environmental Ethics* (New York: Oxford University Press, 2017) 51 at 57.

15 Michael M'Gonigle and Paula Ramsay, "Greening Environmental Law: From Sectoral Reform to Systemic Re-formation" (2004) 14 J Envtl L Prac 333; Geoffrey Garver, *Ecological Law and the Planetary Crisis: A Legal Guide for Harmony on Earth* (London: Routledge, 2020) at 23, 104; Gregorio M Cuadros, "Environmental Rights, Responsibility and Care: A New Constitutional Paradigm" in Jordi Jaria-Manzano and Susana Borrás, eds, *Research Handbook on Global Climate Constitutionalism* (Cheltenham: Edward Elgar, 2019) 176 at 177–80 [Jaria-Manzano and Borrás, *Research Handbook*].

16 See e.g. Jason MacLean, "You Say You Want an Environmental Rights Revolution: Try Changing Canadians' Minds Instead (of the *Charter*)" (2018) 49:1 Ottawa L Rev 183.

17 See e.g. David R Boyd, *The Environmental Rights Revolution: A Global Study of Constitutions, Human Rights, and the Environment* (Vancouver: UBC Press, 2012) at 287 [Boyd, *Environmental Rights Revolution*].

18 *Ibid*; Chris Jeffords and Joshua C Gellers, "Constitutionalizing Environmental Rights: A Practical Guide" (2017) 9: J Hum Rts Prac 136; Christopher Jeffords and Lanse Minkler, "Do Constitutions Matter? The Effect of Constitutional Environmental Rights Provisions on

Environmental Outcomes: Constitutions and the Environment" (2016) 69:2 Kyklos 294.

19 Klaus Bosselmann, "Property Rights and Sustainability: Can They Be Reconciled?" in David P Grinlinton and Prue Taylor, eds, *Property Rights and Sustainability: The Evolution of Property Rights to Meet Ecological Challenges* (Leiden: Martinus Nijhoff, 2011) 21 at 26 [emphasis in original].

20 *Hunter v Southam*, [1984] 2 SCR 145 at para 16.

21 See generally Benjamin J Richardson, *Time and Environmental Law: Telling Nature's Time* (Cambridge: Cambridge University Press, 2017).

22 *Ibid.*

23 See Bosselmann, *Principle of Sustainability*, *supra* note 1 at 12, 166.

24 Boyd, *Environmental Rights Revolution*, *supra* note 17 at 4.

25 David Takacs, "We Are the River" (2020) U Ill L Rev (forthcoming).

26 Louis J Kotzé, "Sustainable Development and the Rule of Law for Nature: A Constitutional Reading" in Christina Voigt, ed., *Rule of Law for Nature: New Dimensions and Ideas in Environmental Law* (Cambridge: Cambridge University Press, 2013) 130 at 130–45.

27 Jordi Jaria-Manzano and Susana Borrás, "Introduction to the *Research Handbook on Global Climate Constitutionalism*" in Jaria-Manzano and Borrás, *Research Handbook*, *supra* note 15, 1 at 4.

28 The Right Honourable Beverley McLachlin, "Lord Cooke of Thorndon Lecture – Unwritten Constitutional Principles: What Is Going On?" (2006) 4:2 NZ J Pub Intl L 147 at 151.

29 James R May and Erin Daly, *Global Environmental Constitutionalism* (Cambridge: Cambridge University Press, 2014) at 1.

30 Louis J Kotzé, "A Global Environmental Constitution for the Anthropocene's Climate Crisis" in Jaria-Manzano and Borrás, *Research Handbook*, *supra* note 15, 50 at 52.

31 Bosselmann, *Principle of Sustainability*, *supra* note 1 at 166.

32 *Harmony with Nature: Report of the Secretary General*, UNGA, 74th session, UN DOC A/74/236 (2019) at para 133.

33 Louis J Kotzé, "Arguing Global Environmental Constitutionalism" (2012)1:1 Transnat'l Envtl L 199 at 224.

34 *Ibid.*

35 Boyd, *Environmental Rights Revolution*, *supra* note 17 at 93.

36 *Constitution of the Democratic People's Republic of Korea* (1972, revised 2016) at article 57 (emphasis added).

37 *Constitution of Ukraine* (1996) at article 16; *Constitution of the Islamic Republic of Afghanistan* (26 January 2004) at article 15.

38 *Constitution of the Kingdom of Norway* (17 May 1814, most recently amended 14 May 2020) at article 112.

39 *Constitution of Albania* (21 October 1998) at article 59(1)(dh).

40 Carla Sbert, *The Lens of Ecological Law: A Look at Mining* (Cheltenham: Edward Elgar, 2020).

41 "Algerians Approve New Constitution After Referendum", *Al Jazeera* (13 November 2020) <https://www.aljazeera.com/news/2020/11/13/algerias-new-constitution-approved-official-results-show>.

42 *2020 Draft of the Constitution of Algeria* (30 May 2020) at article 67.

43 *Constitution of Algeria* (1989, reinstated in 1996 with amendments through 2016) at article 68.
44 *Constitution of the Republic of Seychelles* (21 June 1993) at article 38.
45 *Constitution of the Republic of South Africa*, Art. 24.
46 Anél du Plessis, "The Promise of 'Well-Being' in Article 24 of the Constitution of South Africa" (2018) 34:2 SAJHR 191 at 201. See also Stefan Theil, "The Problem with the Normative Content of Section 24 of the Constitution of South Africa" (2019) 37:2 Nordic J Hum Rts 105.
47 See Sbert, *supra* note 40 at 170–1.
48 *Ibid* at 171.
49 Ashish Kothari, Federico Demaria and Alberto Acosta, "Buen Vivir, Degrowth and Ecological Swaraj: Alternatives to Sustainable Development and the Green Economy" (2015) 57 Development 362 at 370, cited in Sbert, *supra* note 40 at 71.
50 *Constitution of 2008 of the Republic of Ecuador* (20 October 2008) at preamble, articles 3, 14, 26, 32, 74, 83, 97, 250, 258, 275.
51 *Constitution of 2009 of the Plurinational State of Bolivia* (9 February 2009) at article 8.
52 Corte Constitucional del Ecuador [Constitutional Court of Ecuador], 20 May 2015, *Sentencia No. 166-15-SEP-CC*, Caso No. 0507-12-EP.
53 James R May and Erin Daly, "Six Trends in Global Environmental Constitutionalism" (2018) Environmental Constitutionalism: Impact on Legal Systems? at 60 (Oxford: Peter Lang Publishing).
54 United Nations Special Rapporteur on the Issue of Human Rights Obligations Relating to the Enjoyment of a Safe, Clean, Healthy and Sustainable Environment, *Right to A Healthy Environment: Good Practices*, OHCHR, 43rd session, UN DOC A/HRC/43/53 at paras 9-13.
55 See e.g. Ian Greene, "Constitutional Amendment in Canada and the United States" in Stephen L Newman, ed., *Constitutional Politics in Canada and the United States* (Albany: SUNY Press, 2004) 249; Joel I Colón Ríos, "The Counter-Majoritarian Difficulty and the Road Not Taken: Democratizing Amendment Rules" (2012) 25:1 Can JL Jur 53.
56 See *Minors Oposa v Secretary of the Department of Environment and Natural Resources* (1993), 33 ILM 173 (1994) (Supreme Court of the Philippines) at 187.
57 *Juliana v United States*, 217 F Supp (3d) 1224 at 1250 (D Or 2016).
58 *Ibid* (internal citations omitted).
59 Lynda Collins and Lorne Sossin, "In Search of an Ecological Approach to Constitutional Principles and Environmental Discretion in Canada" (2019) 52:1 UBC L Rev 293.
60 See Sumudu Attapatu, "Environmental Justice, Climate Justice and Constitutionalism: Protecting Vulnerable States and Communities" in Jaria-Manzano and Borrás, *Research Handbook, supra* note 15 195.
61 *Tsilhqot'in Nation v. British Columbia*, [2014] 2 SCR 257, 2014 SCC 44 at para 86.
62 John Borrows, "Earth-Bound: Indigenous Resurgence and Environmental Reconciliation" in Michael Asch, John Borrows and James Tully, eds, *Resurgence and Reconciliation: Indigenous-Settler Relations and Earth Teachings* (Toronto: University of Toronto Press, 2018) 49 at 49–50 [Borrows, "Earth-Bound"]; Benjamin J Richardson, "The Ties

That Bind: Indigenous Peoples and Environmental Governance" in Benjamin J Richardson, Shin Imai and Kent McNeil, eds, *Indigenous Peoples and the Law: Comparative and Critical Perspectives* (Oxford: Hart Publishing, 2009).

63 See e.g. *Richardson, supra* note 61; *Borrows*, "Earth-Bound", *supra* note 61. See also John Borrows, "Living Law on a Living Earth: Aboriginal Religion, Law, and the Constitution" in Richard Moon, ed., *Law and Religious Pluralism in Canada* (Vancouver: UBC Press, 2008) 161; Elizabeth Ann Kronk Warner, "Tribes as Innovative Environmental 'Laboratories'" (2015) 86:3 U Colo L Rev 789.

64 See e.g. Rebecca A Tsosie, "Climate Change, Sustainability, and Globalization: Charting the Future of Indigenous Environmental Self-Determination" (2009) 4:2 Envlt Energy L Pol'y J 188.

65 *Report of the Special Rapporteur on the Issue of Human Rights Obligations Relating to the Enjoyment of a Safe, Clean, Healthy and Sustainable Environment*, OHCHR, 73rd session, UN DOC A/73/188 (2018).

References

"Algerians Approve New Constitution After Referendum", *Al Jazeera* (13 November 2020) <https://www.aljazeera.com/news/2020/11/13/algerias-new-constitution-approved-official-results-show>.

Adelman, Sam, "The Sustainable Development Goals, Anthropocentrism and Neoliberalism" in Duncan French & Louis J Kotzé, eds, *Sustainable Development Goals: Law, Theory and Implementation* (Northampton, MA: Edward Elgar, 2018) 15.

Attapatu, Sumudu, "Environmental Justice, Climate Justice and Constitutionalism: Protecting Vulnerable States and Communities" in Jordi Jaria-Manzano & Susana Borrás, eds, *Research Handbook on Climate Constitutionalism* (Cheltenham: Edward Elgar, 2019) 195.

Borrows, John, "Earth-Bound: Indigenous Law and Environmental Reconciliation" in Michael Asch, John Borrows & James Tully, eds, *Resurgence and Reconciliation: Indigenous-Settler Relations and Earth Teachings* (Toronto: University of Toronto Press, 2018) 49.

Borrows, John, "Living Law on a Living Earth: Aboriginal Religion, Law, and the Constitution" in Richard Moon, ed., *Law and Religious Pluralism in Canada* (Vancouver: UBC Press, 2008) 161.

Bosselmann, Klaus, *The Principle of Sustainability: Transforming Law and Governance*, 2nd ed. (London: Routledge, 2016).

Bosselmann, Klaus, "Property Rights and Sustainability: Can They Be Reconciled?" in David P Grinlinton & Prue Taylor, eds, *Property Rights and Sustainability: The Evolution of Property Rights to Meet Ecological Challenges* (Leiden: Martinus Nijhoff, 2011) 21.

Boyd, David R, *The Environmental Rights Revolution: A Global Study of Constitutions, Human Rights, and the Environment* (Vancouver: UBC Press, 2012).

Boyd, David R, *Report of the Special Rapporteur on the Issue of Human Rights Obligations Relating to the Enjoyment of a Safe, Clean, Healthy and Sustainable Environment*, OHCHR, 75th session, UN DOC A/75/161 (2020).

Boyd, David R, "Sustainability Law: (R)Evolutionary Directions for the Future of Environmental Law" (2004) 14 J Envtl L Prac 357.

Bratspies, Rebecca M, "Sustainability: Can Law Meet the Challenge?" (2011) 34:2 Suffolk Transnat'l L Rev 283.

Butt, Daniel, "Law, Governance, and the Ecological Ethos" in Stephen M Gardiner & Allen Thompson, eds, *The Oxford Handbook of Environmental Ethics* (New York: Oxford University Press, 2017) 51.

Collins, Lynda M, "Revisiting the Doctrine of Intergenerational Equity in Global Environmental Governance" (2007) 30:1 Dal LJ 79.

Collins, Lynda M, "The Unwritten Constitutional Principle of Ecological Sustainability: A Solution to the Pipelines Puzzle?" (2019) 70 UNBLJ 30.

Constitution of 2008 of the Republic of Ecuador (20 October 2008).

Constitution of 2009 of the Plurinational State of Bolivia (9 February 2009).

Constitution of Albania (21 October 1998).

Constitution of Algeria (1989, reinstated in 1996 with amendments through 2016).

Constitution of the Democratic People's Republic of Korea (1972, revised 2016).

Constitution of the Islamic Republic of Afghanistan (26 January 2004).

Constitution of the Kingdom of Norway (17 May 1814, most recently amended 14 May 2020).

Constitution of the Republic of Seychelles (21 June 1993).

Constitution of Ukraine (1996).

Corte Constitucional del Ecuador [Constitutional Court of Ecuador], 20 May 2015, *Sentencia No. 166-15-SEP-CC*, Caso No. 0507-12-EP.

Cuadros, Gregorio M, "Environmental Rights, Responsibility and Care: A New Constitutional Paradigm" in Jordi Jaria-Manzano & Susana Borrás, eds, *Research Handbook on Global Climate Constitutionalism* (Cheltenham: Edward Elgar, 2019) 176.

Draft Constitution of Algeria (1 November 2020).

Garver, Geoffrey, *Ecological Law and the Planetary Crisis: A Legal Guide for Harmony on Earth* (London: Routledge, 2020).

Greene, Ian, "Constitutional Amendment in Canada and the United States" in Stephen L. Newman, ed., *Constitutional Politics in Canada and the United States* (Albany: SUNY Press, 2004) 249.

Harmony with Nature: Report of the UN Secretary General, UNGAOR, 72nd Session, UN Doc A/72/175 (2017).

Hunter v Southam, [1984] 2 SCR 145, 11 DLR (4th) 641.

Jaria-Manzano, Jordi & Susana Borrás, "Introduction to the *Research Handbook on Global Climate Constitutionalism*" in Jordi Jaria-Manzano & Susana Borrás, eds, *Research Handbook on Climate Constitutionalism* (Cheltenham: Edward Elgar, 2019) 1.

Jeffords, Chris & Joshua C Gellers, "Constitutionalizing Environmental Rights: A Practical Guide" (2017) 9: J Hum Rts Prac 136.

Jeffords, Christopher & Lanse Minkler, "Do Constitutions Matter? The Effect of Constitutional Environmental Rights Provisions on Environmental Outcomes: Constitutions and the Environment" (2016) 69:2 Kyklos 294.

Juliana v United States, 217 F Supp (3d) 1224 (D Or 2016).

Kim, Rakhyun E & Klaus Bosselmann, "Operationalizing Sustainable Development: Ecological Integrity as a Grundnorm of International Law" (2015) 24:2 RECIEL 194.

Kothari, Ashish, Federico Demaria & Alberto Acosta, "Buen Vivir, Degrowth and Ecological Swaraj: Alternatives to Sustainable Development and the Green Economy" (2015) 57 Development 362.

Kotzé, Louis J, "Arguing Global Environmental Constitutionalism" (2012) 1:1 Transnat'l Envtl L 199.

Kotzé, Louis J, "A Global Environmental Constitution for the Anthropocene's Climate Crisis" in Jordi Jaria-Manzano & Susana Borrás, eds, *Research Handbook on Climate Constitutionalism* (Cheltenham: Edward Elgar, 2019) 50 at 74.

Kotzé, Louis J, "Sustainable Development and the Rule of Law for Nature: A Constitutional Reading" in Christina Voigt, ed., *Rule of Law for Nature: New Dimensions and Ideas in Environmental Law* (Cambridge: Cambridge University Press, 2013) 130.

LaFollette, Cameron & Chris Maser, *Sustainability and the Rights of Nature: An Introduction* (Boca Raton, FL: CRC Press, 2017).

MacLean, Jason, "You Say You Want an Environmental Rights Revolution: Try Changing Canadians' Minds Instead (of the *Charter*)" (2018) 49:1 Ottawa L Rev 183.

May, James R & Erin Daly, *Global Environmental Constitutionalism* (Cambridge: Cambridge University Press, 2014).

May, James R & Erin Daly, "Six Trends in Global Environmental Constitutionalism" in Jochen Sohnle, ed, Environmental Constitutionalism: Impact on Legal Systems? (Paris: Peter Lang, 2019) 45–66.

McLachlin, The Right Honourable Beverley, "Lord Cooke of Thorndon Lecture – Unwritten Constitutional Principles: What Is Going On?" (2006) 4:2 NZ J Pub Intl L 147.

M'Gonigle, Michael & Paula Ramsay, "Greening Environmental Law: From Sectoral Reform to Systemic Re-formation" (2004) 14 J Envtl L Prac 333.

Plessis, Anél du, "The Promise of 'Well-Being' in Article 24 of the Constitution of South Africa" (2018) 34:2 SAJHR 191.

Report of the Special Rapporteur on the Issue of Human Rights Obligations Relating to the Enjoyment of a Safe, Clean, Healthy and Sustainable Environment: Right to a Healthy Environment: Good Practices, OHCHR, 43rd Session, UN Doc A/HRC/43/53 (2020).

Report of the Special Rapporteur on the Issue of Human Rights Obligations Relating to the Enjoyment of a Safe, Clean, Healthy and Sustainable Environment: Safe Climate, OHCHR, 73rd Session, UN Doc A/73/188 (2018).

Richardson, Benjamin J, "The Ties That Bind: Indigenous Peoples and Environmental Governance" in Benjamin J Richardson, Shin Imai & Kent McNeil, eds, *Indigenous Peoples and the Law: Comparative and Critical Perspectives* (Oxford: Hart Publishing, 2009) 337.

Richardson, Benjamin J, *Time and Environmental Law: Telling Nature's Time* (Cambridge: Cambridge University Press, 2017).

Ríos, Joel I C, "The Counter-Majoritarian Difficulty and the Road Not Taken: Democratizing Amendment Rules" (2012) 25:1 Can JL Jur 53.

Sbert, Carla, *The Lens of Ecological Law: A Look at Mining* (Cheltenham: Edward Elgar, 2020).

Takacs, David, "We Are the River" (2021) 2 U Ill L Rev 545.

Theil, Stefan, "The Problem with the Normative Content of Section 24 of the Constitution of South Africa" (2019) 37:2 Nordic J Hum Rts 105.

Tsilhqot'in Nation v British Columbia, 2014 SCC 44.

Tsosie, Rebecca A, "Climate Change, Sustainability, and Globalization: Charting the Future of Indigenous Environmental Self-Determination" (2009) 4:2 Environ Energy L Policy J 188.

Warner, Elizabeth AK, "Tribes as Innovative Environmental 'Laboratories'" (2015) 86:3 U Colo L Rev 789.

Woolley, Olivia, *Ecological Governance: Reappraising Law's Role in Protecting Ecosystem Functionality* (Cambridge: Cambridge University Press, 2014).

3 Human rights in the ecological constitution

As Mesa Cuadros reminds us, "...rights are nothing more than socially shared meanings. They do not fall from the sky and are not affirmed in a day; they are the result of lengthy processes through which their normative statements consolidate in the collective consciousness".[1] The recognition of environmental rights as the ancestor and prerequisite to all other human rights has now taken hold in the legal consciousness of governments, courts and civil society around the world. Indeed, from an ecologically literate perspective, the right to environment may be seen as the primary, irreducible, human right.[2] Recent decades have seen a rapid global expansion of rights-based approaches to environmental protection that Boyd has appropriately termed an "environmental rights revolution".[3]

This chapter will explore four distinct streams of environmental human rights that are relevant to ecological constitutionalism: (i) procedural environmental rights; (ii) the protection of pre-existing human rights from environmental deprivations; (iii) the freestanding substantive right to a "safe, clean, healthy and sustainable environment"[4]; and (iv) the unique environmental rights of Indigenous peoples.[5] A final topic to be considered is the potential for ecological imperatives to constrain existing human rights.

Procedural environmental rights

Procedural environmental rights (PERs) include access to information, the right to participate and access to justice in environmental matters. The constitutions of at least 40 nations specifically include protection for at least one category of such rights.[6] Colombia's right to a healthy environment, for example, includes a provision requiring legislation to "guarantee the community's participation in the decisions that may affect it".[7] The Czech Republic's constitution states that "[e]verybody is entitled to timely and complete information about the state of the environment and natural resources",[8] and Ecuador's constitution includes several provisions allowing individuals and groups access to courts and administrative agencies to enforce environmental human rights and the rights of nature.[9]

In a compelling 2018 empirical analysis, Gellers and Jeffords conclude that "constitutionally entrenched PERs, specifically those relating to information, are positively associated with environmental justice outcomes [ie] a more equitable distribution of environmental goods".[10] Along with strong protection for civil and political rights,[11] PERs make it easier for activists to advocate for ecological outcomes and, therefore, merit inclusion in an ecological constitution.

Environmental dimensions of pre-existing rights

The pre-existing rights approach recognises that serious state-sponsored environmental harm[12] can violate recognised rights such as the rights to life, dignity, personal security, equality, privacy and family life, culture, religion and health (among others).[13] Multiple constitutional courts around the world have recognised environmental deprivations of existing rights. In one environmental claim, for example, the Supreme Court of Pakistan held that "[a]ny action taken which may create hazards of life will be encroaching upon the person rights of a citizen to enjoy the life according to law".[14] The Indian Supreme Court has gone further, holding that "[t]he right to life ... includes the right of enjoyment of pollution-free water and air for full enjoyment of life".[15] Nigeria's Federal High Court has similarly declared that the right to life enshrined in that country's constitution "inevitably" includes the right to a "clean, poison-free, healthy environment".[16]

Although some commentators advance the idea of "greening human rights law",[17] it is equally possible to accept existing rights as they are currently understood and simply adopt an ecologically literate approach to rights infringement. Indeed, to deny a constitutional remedy for state-sponsored environmental deprivations of recognised rights would in effect be to create an irrational exception in rights protection. As I have written elsewhere,

> ...it may be as simple as recognizing that an individual who is killed by a state-permitted air emission is equally dead as one who is shot by state police. Both should be protected from the

deprivation of life, even though the former death is mediated by environmental forces while the latter is not.[18]

The substantive right to a safe, clean, healthy and sustainable environment

Although environmental interests may find protection through judicial interpretation of other rights, best practice in this area is the explicit recognition of a substantive environmental right that not only encompasses but also extends beyond the content of existing rights, such as the right to life.[19] Indeed,

> [i]n some ... countries, including Argentina, Brazil, Colombia, Costa Rica, France, the Philippines, Portugal, and South Africa, the right to a healthy environment has systematically transformed the environmental legal system, providing a unifying goal that all laws and policies are restructured to achieve.[20]

The domestic constitutions of at least 110 states include a substantive environmental right variously described as the right to a "healthy", "clean", "safe", "sound", "adequate" and/or "ecologically balanced" environment (among other formulations).[21] The right to environment may also be found in multiple subnational constitutions.[22]

Some constitutional environmental rights provisions are very concise, such as Article 51 of Chad's 2018 Constitution, which states simply: "Every person has the right to a healthy environment".[23] Others are much more detailed, as in the case of Ecuador, whose constitution recognises "[t]he right of the population to live in a healthy and ecologically balanced environment that guarantees sustainability and the good way of living (sumak kawsay)".[24] This provision is further elaborated and complemented by a myriad of others addressing environmental education,[25] the right to water,[26] the right to health (which the State is required to guarantee through inter alia "environmental policies")[27] and the rights of nature.[28] Dozens of national constitutions similarly recognise the right to water, which has its own status and content in international law.[29]

In his ground-breaking 2012 book, *The Environmental Rights Revolution*, Boyd demonstrates that constitutional codification of environmental rights produces significant improvements in environmental legislation, environmental litigation outcomes and, most importantly, environmental performance.[30] These benefits are seen across a diverse range of political contexts, including both developing and developed countries with constitutions ranging from very new to very old.

The data are compelling: compared to countries that lack such protection, nations with constitutional environmental rights rank higher on multi-indicator assessments of environmental performance, have smaller "ecological footprints" (a comprehensive measurement of environmental impact) and have been more successful in reducing dangerous air pollutants, including greenhouse gases.[31] These relative improvements apply regardless whether nations are compared with all other countries around the globe or with only those in their own region (e.g. Africa, the Americas, Asia-Pacific, Europe and the Middle East/Central Asia).[32]

More recent research confirms Boyd's findings; for example, a 2016 study by Jeffords and Minkler reports that "the presence and legal strength of existing constitutional environmental rights provisions, in particular substantive environmental rights provisions, are positively associated with environmental outcomes as measured by Yale's Environmental Performance Index".[33] Further research by Jeffords notes specifically that "there is a positive and statistically significant relationship between [constitutional environmental rights] provisions and access to improved drinking water sources".[34]

Despite empirical evidence of its efficacy, the right to a healthy environment is not without its critics. Human rights-based approaches to environmental protection have been challenged as anthropocentric, Eurocentric, neo-colonialist, ineffective, poorly understood or even counterproductive.[35] Some constitutional formulations of environmental human rights arguably fail all three criteria of Carla Sbert's "lens of ecological law" (ecocentrism, ecological primacy and ecological justice).[36] Thus, one might reasonably question why an ecological constitution would include environmental human rights.

Kotzé and Villavicencio Calzadilla summarise the main concerns raised by critics:

> [A]nthropocentric law and its embedded juridical constructs of rights ... have become tools that legally create human entitlements to the environment, that justify and legitimize these entitlements, and that strengthen them through laying (in most instances constitutional) claims to the environment and its benefits to human development as of right.... Such a resolutely

anthropocentric ideological orientation of rights is seen to allow, legitimize and reinforce the type of unrestricted anthropocentric behaviour that many now believe is pushing Earth into ... the Anthropocene [era].[37]

It is certainly possible to approach environmental human rights from an anthropocentric perspective that fails to challenge the kind of binary thinking that has led to our current ecological crises. However, while the most obvious application of environmental human rights involves pollution affecting human health, the "right to a healthy environment" should "be understood as encompassing both human-centred and eco-centric aspects – as in an environment that is both 'healthy' for humans and healthy in its own right (e.g. a healthy lake, a healthy forest, a healthy ecosystem)"[38]. Indeed, it has become patently clear that the enjoyment of environmental human rights depends upon a healthy biosphere.

In his most recent report to the UN, the Special Rapporteur on Human Rights and the Environment states clearly that "[h]ealthy ecosystems and biodiversity are substantive elements of the [human] right to a healthy environment, as recognized by regional tribunals, national laws and national jurisprudence".[39] Other substantive elements of this right that are consistent with an ecological approach include "a safe climate, clean air, clean water and nontoxic environments".[40] To clarify the broad scope of environmental human rights, the current UN Special Rapporteur on Human Rights and the Environment has adopted the formulation "right to a safe, clean, healthy and sustainable environment".[41]

A substantial number of domestic constitutions already employ a holistic approach to rights-based environmental protection, blurring the lines between anthropocentrism and ecocentrism. Bhutan, Brazil, Cape Verde, Costa Rica, the Dominican Republic, Ecuador, Maldives, Paraguay, Portugal, Timor-Leste and Venezuela, all include the notion of ecological balance in their substantive environmental rights provisions. The 2015 Constitution of the Dominican Republic, for example, recognises the right "to live in an environment that is healthy, ecologically balanced, and adequate for the development and preservation of the different forms of life, scenery and nature".[42] Similarly, the constitution of Timor-Leste provides that "[a]ll have the right to a humane, healthy, and ecologically balanced environment and the duty to protect it and improve it for the benefit of the future generations".[43] In addition to this kind of textual guidance, "[c]ourts in all regions of the world have determined that the failure of States to take adequate action to protect healthy ecosystems and biodiversity can violate the right to a healthy environment".[44]

Finally, it should be noted that even an anthropocentric conception of the right to a healthy environment is highly relevant to sustainability since there is a massive overlap in the ecological needs of human and other natural beings (e.g. clean air, clean water, biodiversity). In societies in which "[t]he language of rights now dominates political debate",[45] creating and enforcing environmental human rights may be a highly effective way to encourage ordinary people to demand ecological decision-making from their governments. Most importantly, the empirical data confirm that such rights make a difference on the ground, improving ecological health for all species. Thus, while environmental human rights may or may not form part of the cannon of ecological law, they undoubtedly advance the cause of ecological sustainability.

Indigenous environmental rights

In addition to generally applicable constitutional environmental rights enjoyed by all citizens/residents of a given nation, it is well established that Indigenous individuals and communities have unique environmental rights.[46] Article 29(1) of the United Nations Declaration on the Rights of Indigenous Peoples, for example, provides that "Indigenous peoples have the right to the conservation and protection of the environment and the productive capacity of their lands or territories and resources".[47]

The Declaration also protects Indigenous rights to "maintain, protect, and have access in privacy" to sacred sites; the right "to maintain and strengthen their distinctive spiritual relationship with their [traditional territories] and to uphold their responsibilities to future generations in this regard"[48]; the right to "conservation of ... vital medicinal plants, animals and minerals"[49]; and "the right to determine and develop priorities and strategies for the development or use of their lands or territories and other resources".[50] The ecological interests of Indigenous peoples require constitutional protection for at least three interrelated reasons.

First, around the world, Indigenous peoples bear an unbalanced share of environmental burdens compared to their non-Indigenous counterparts.[51] Indigenous peoples disproportionately suffer the destructive impacts of hazardous waste disposal and extractive industries including mining, logging, unsustainable agriculture, hydroelectric development and the like.[52] Conversely, Indigenous communities rarely share equitably in the economic benefits derived from such activities.[53] Moreover, Indigenous activists are particularly vulnerable to human rights abuses in response to their opposition to destructive developments in their territories.[54]

Second, though Indigenous peoples are not monolithic and cannot be essentialised as uniformly ecological actors,[55] Indigenous peoples do enjoy a unique relationship with their traditional territories.[56] In many cases, members of Indigenous communities engage in subsistence and/or commercial resource-based activities such as hunting, fishing and trapping, which place them in a direct relationship of dependence on land and resources.[57] Moreover, connection with and stewardship of the land is a central organising principle in many Indigenous belief systems. As one Indigenous commentator has written, "[t]he First Nations' relationships with the land have always defined their identity, their spiritual ecology, and their reality".[58] In stark contrast to Western worldviews which commodify land and define its worth according to human use-value, many Indigenous cosmologies find inherent "value *in* the world, and in relationships properly maintained with the land".[59]

Third, Indigenous legal systems have crystallised these worldviews in effective governance systems that could assist governments at all levels in achieving sustainability. While it is important to avoid romantic stereotypes that may essentialise or constrain Indigenous peoples,[60] there is no doubt much to be learned from historic and contemporary Indigenous approaches to environmental protection.[61] Historically, environmental law around the world has failed to appreciate the contributions of Indigenous legal systems. Borrows observes that "[Indigenous] knowledge has often been delegitimated and thus concealed from wider public view. So-called 'democratic' institutions repress Indigenous participation, degrade their environments, and thereby hinder the extension of knowledge about how to coexist with the environment".[62] In the ecologically constitutional state, Indigenous ecological rights would extend beyond environmental quality to encompass rights of self-governance in ecological matters.[63]

Ecological self-governance gives Indigenous peoples the ability to implement their own law and cosmovision, as was famously accomplished in New Zealand, where a river, volcano and mountain ecosystem were recognised as legal persons with stewardship to be carried out by Maori-led bodies according to Maori law and traditional knowledge[64]; Ecuador, where the 2008 constitution enshrines the Indigenous concept of *sumak kawsay*, or "living well" and recognises the rights of Pacha Mama, or Mother Earth[65]; and Columbia, where the courts have recognised "bio-cultural rights" integrating both the inherent rights of nature and the rights of communities who live with and from the natural world.[66] The Supreme Court of Columbia explains:

> [B]iocultural rights, in their simplest definition, refer to the rights that ethnic communities have to administer and exercise autonomous guardianship over their territories – according to their own laws and customs – and the natural resources that make up their habitat, where their culture, their traditions and their way of life are developed based on the special relationship they have with the environment and biodiversity.[67]

Ecological limits on rights

Since human rights are both central to constitutions and interdependent and indivisible, constitutional approaches to ecological sustainability can never countenance the violation of fundamental human rights to achieve ecological outcomes (e.g. through coercive population control measures or the forced displacement of Indigenous peoples from conservation areas). Indeed, human rights are an integral component of intra-generational equity, environmental democracy and Indigenous rights, which are widely recognised as tenets of ecological law.[68] However, while human rights and ecological protection are fundamentally mutually enhancing, tensions will sometimes arise between the two.

Chapter 6 of this volume elaborates on the delicate balance between rights of nature and human rights, but the central idea is that both categories must be weighed and considered by decision-makers at all levels. In most cases, ecological protection advances the whole range of human rights discussed above. Where irreconcilable micro-conflicts arise in specific cases, courts can employ their usual justificatory tests for rights limitations,[69] supplemented by newer policy tools such as Winter's framework for eco-proportionality.[70] Fortunately, it is now abundantly clear that development pathways exist to meet the human rights to life, work, food, water, housing and an adequate standard of living in ecologically sustainable ways.[71]

Occasionally, there can be conflict between environmental rights of present and future generations, e.g. where "groundwater mining" is employed to satisfy current humans' right to water, to the detriment of future humans' ability to do the same.[72] Again, such conflicts can usually be avoided by the adoption of sustainable life-ways,[73] systems and technologies. Where the conflict is complex, it may be addressed through the doctrine of intergenerational equity, which involves a sophisticated balancing of the rights of present and future generations of humans and is discussed in the next chapter.

The most obvious and morally defensible application of ecological limitations to human rights pertains to property rights, particularly in the developed world.[74] The commodification of nature and its complete subjection to private and public ownership are arguably at the very root of our current ecological crisis.[75] It is no surprise, then, that ecological law thinkers challenge the sanctity of property rights.[76] Thomas Berry, for example, argues that:

> Human property rights are not absolute. Property rights are simply a special relationship between a particular human 'owner' and a particular piece of 'property' so that both might fulfill their roles in the great community of existence.[77]

More than a dozen domestic constitutions include provisions explicitly subjecting property rights to ecological limitations, and many more authorise the infringement of property rights in the general public interest.[78] Romania's constitution, for example, provides that "[t]he right to own property implies an obligation to comply with duties relating to environmental protection".[79] Bolivia's constitution guarantees the right to hold private property provided that "that the use made of it is not harmful to the collective interests".[80] In Germany, constitutional recognition of the state's responsibility to protect "the natural foundations of life" has led to a legal understanding that property ownership includes inherent environmental obligations.[81]

Bosselmann affirms that sustainability and property rights can and must be reconciled, but this process will require a radical revision of worldviews and resulting legal systems. In particular, he argues that "*inherent* limitations to property rights" flow from the realisation that "...land use plays a role in controlling the global climate and biodiversity and that it holds the key for the capacity of a nation or region to sustain itself".[82] Thus, it is both logical and necessary for an ecologically literate constitution to recognise explicit limitations on property rights, particularly where such rights are themselves constitutionally protected.

Notes

1 Gregorio M Cuadros, "Environmental Rights, Responsibility and Care: A New Constitutional Paradigm" in Jordi Jaria-Manzano and Susana Borrás, eds, *Research Handbook on Climate Constitutionalism* (London: Edward Elgar, 2019) at 181, citing Luigi Ferrajoli, *Derechos y garantías. La ley del más débil* (Madrid: Trotta, 1999) at 54.

2 See *Minors Oposa v Secretary of the Department of Environment and Natural Resources* (1993), 33 ILM 173 at 187.

3 David R Boyd, *The Environmental Rights Revolution: A Global Study of Constitutions, Human Rights, and the Environment* (Vancouver: University of British Columbia Press, 2012) [Boyd, "The Environmental Rights Revolution"].

4 *Report of the Special Rapporteur on the Issue of Human Rights Obligations Relating to the Enjoyment of a Safe, Clean, Healthy and Sustainable Environment: Safe Climate*, OHCHR, 73rd Session, UN Doc A/73/188 (2018) [OHCHR, "Safe Climate"].

5 *Ibid.* See also Dinah Shelton and Donald K Anton, *Environmental Protection and Human Rights* (Cambridge: Cambridge University Press, 2011); Dinah Shelton, *Human Rights and the Environment* (Cheltenham: Edward Elgar Publishing, 2011); Lynda M Collins, "Are We There Yet? The Right to Environment in International and European Law" (2007) 3:2 JSDLP 119 [Collins, "Are We There Yet?"].

6 Joshua C Gellers and Chris Jeffords, "Towards Environmental Democracy? Procedural Environmental Rights and Environmental Justice" (2018) 18 Global Envtl Polit 99 at 108.

7 *Political Constitution of the Republic of Colombia* (4 July 1991) at art 79.

8 *Constitution of the Czech Republic* (16 December 1992) at art 35(2).

9 See e.g. *Constitution of Ecuador* (10 August 2008) at arts 11, 74, 75.

10 Gellers and Jeffords, *supra* note 6 at 116.

11 See e.g. John H Knox, "Human Rights, Environmental Protection and the Sustainable Development Goals" (2015) 24 Wash Intl L J 517.

12 States create environmental harm through their own direct conduct (e.g. state-owned mining and power plants), by issuing affirmative permits for pollution or unsustainable resource extraction to private parties, by setting inadequate statutory standards (e.g. pollution regulations that allow unsafe levels of air pollution, environmental assessment regimes that fail to capture climate change impacts) and by chronic failure to enforce environmental laws. See Lynda M Collins, "An Ecologically Literate Reading of the *Canadian Charter of Rights and Freedoms*" (2009) 26:1 Windsor Rev Legal Soc Issues 7.

13 See Shelton and Anton, *supra* note 5; Collins, *supra* note 5 at 128.

14 *Zia v WAPDA*, [1994] PLD SC 693 (Pakistan).

15 *Subhash Kumar v State of Bihar et al*, [1991] AIR 420, 1991 SCR (1) 5 (India). WP (Civil) No 381 of 1988, D/-9-1-91 (India). See also *MC Mehta v India*, [1985] WP (Civil) No 12739 of 1985 (India); *Indian Council for Enviro-Legal Action v Union of India*, [1996] 5 Supreme Court Cases 281 (India), per Kuldip Singh J; Jona Razzaque, *Public Interest Environmental Litigation in India, Pakistan, and Bangladesh* (The Hague: Kluwer Law International, 2004) at 87 *et seq.*

16 *Gbemre v Shell Petroleum Development Co Nigeria Ltd*, [2005] FHC/B/
    CS/53/05 (Nigeria). See Kaniye SA Ebeku, "Constitutional Right to a
    Healthy Environment and Human Rights Approaches to Environmen-
    tal Protection in Nigeria: *Gbemre v. Shell* Revisited" (2008) 16:3 RE-
    CIEL 312.
17 See e.g. Elina Pirjatanniemi, *Greening Human Rights Law* (London:
    Routledge, 2016); John Lee, "The Underlying Legal Theory to Support a
    Well-Defined Human Right to a Healthy Environment as a Principle of
    Customary International Law" (2000) 25 Colum J Envtl L 238 at 291–2.
18 Collins, *supra* note 12 at 8. See also Louis J Kotzé, "Human Rights and
    the Environment in the Anthropocene" (2014) 1:3 Anthropocene Rev
    252; Lynda M Collins, "The United Nations, Human Rights and the
    Environment" in Louis J Kotzé and Anna Grear, eds, *Research Hand-
    book on Human Rights and the Environment* (London: Edward Elgar,
    2015) 219 at 244.
19 *Report of the Independent Expert on the Issue of Human Rights Obli-
    gations Relating to the Enjoyment of a Safe, Clean, Healthy and Sus-
    tainable Environment, John H. Knox: Compilation of Good Practices*,
    OHCHR, 78th Session, UN Doc A/HRC/28/61 (2015).
20 Lynda M Collins and David Boyd, "Non-Regression and the *Charter*
    Right to a Healthy Environment" (2016) 29 J Envtl L Prac 285 at 292.
21 *Report of the Special Rapporteur on the Issue of Human Rights Obli-
    gations Relating to the Enjoyment of a Safe, Clean, Healthy and Sus-
    tainable Environment: Right to a Healthy Environment: Good Practices*,
    OHCHR, 43rd Session, UN Doc A/HRC/43/53 (2020) at para 10; Boyd,
    "The Environmental Rights Revolution", *supra* note 3 at 59–66.
22 See James R May and Erin Daly, *Global Environmental Constitutional-
    ism* (Cambridge: Cambridge University Press, 2014).
23 *Constitution of the Republic of Chad* (4 May 2018) at art 51.
24 *Constitution of Ecuador* (10 August 2008) at art 14.
25 *Ibid*, art 27.
26 *Ibid*, art 12.
27 *Ibid*, art 32.
28 *Ibid*, arts 71–73.
29 See Norbert Brunner et al., "The Human Right to Water in Law and
    Implementation" (2015) 4:3 Laws 413.
30 Boyd, "The Environmental Rights Revolution", *supra* note 3. See also
    Chris Jeffords and Joshua C Gellers, "Constitutionalizing Environ-
    mental Rights: A Practical Guide" (2017) 9:1 J Hum Rts Prac 136.
31 David R Boyd, *The Right to a Healthy Environment: Revitalizing Cana-
    da's Constitution* (Vancouver: UBC Press, 2015) at 107–21.
32 Boyd, "The Environmental Rights Revolution", *supra* note 3.
33 Jeffords and Gellers, *supra* note 30 at 139.
34 *Ibid* at 140, citing Christopher Jeffords, "On the Temporal Effects of
    Static Constitutional Environmental Rights Provisions on Access to
    Improved Sanitation Facilities and Water Sources" (2016) 7(1) J Hum
    Rts Envtl 74.
35 Anna Grear, "Human Rights and New Horizons: Thoughts toward a
    New Juridical Ontology" (2017) 43:1 Sci Technol Hum Values 129; Jason
    MacLean, "You Say You Want an Environmental Rights Revolution:

Try Changing Canadians Minds Instead (of the *Charter*)" (2018) 49:1 Ottawa L Rev 185; Geoffrey Garver, *Ecological Law and the Planetary Crisis: A Legal Guide for Harmony on Earth* (London: Routledge, 2020) at 104. See also James R May, "The Case for Environmental Human Rights: Recognition, Implementation and Outcomes" (2021) Cardozo L Rev (forthcoming).

36 See e.g. *Constitution of Albania* (26 October 2012) at art 59(1)(dh).

37 Louis J Kotzé and Paola V Calzadilla, "Somewhere between Rhetoric and Reality: Environmental Constitutionalism and the Rights of Nature in Ecuador" (2017) 6:3 Transnat'l Envtl Law 401 at 403.

38 Collins, "Are We There Yet?", *supra* note 5 at 137.

39 *Report of the Special Rapporteur on the Issue of Human Rights Obligations in Relation to the Enjoyment of a Safe, Clean, Healthy and Sustainable Environment: Human Rights Depend on a Healthy Biosphere*, OHCHR, 75th Session, UN Doc A/75/161 (2020) at para 33 [OHCHR, "Human Rights Depend on a Healthy Biosphere"].

40 OHCHR, "Safe Climate", *supra* note 4 at para 43.

41 See, for example, *Ibid.*

42 *Constitution of the Dominican Republic* (13 June 2015) at art 67.

43 *Constitution of the Democratic Republic of Timor-Leste* (20 May 2002) at art 61.

44 OHCHR, "Human Rights Depend on a Healthy Biosphere", *supra* note 40 at para 35. See also *Requested by the Republic of Colombia: The Environment and Human Rights* (2017), Advisory Opinion OC-23/17, Inter-Am Ct HR (Ser A) No 23.

45 See Ronald Dworkin, *Taking Rights Seriously* (Cambridge: Harvard University Press, 1977) at 184.

46 See generally S James Anaya, *Indigenous Peoples in International Law*, 2nd ed. (New York: Oxford University Press, 2004); Cherie Metcalfe, "Indigenous Rights and the Environment: Evolving International Law" (2004) 35:1 Ottawa L Rev 101; Benjamin J Richardson, "The Ties That Bind: Indigenous Peoples and Environmental Governance" in Benjamin J Richardson, Shin Imai and Kent McNeil, eds, *Indigenous Peoples and the Law: Comparative and Critical Perspectives* (Oxford: Hart Publishing, 2009) at 337.

47 *United Nations Declaration on the Rights of Indigenous Peoples*, GA Res 295, UNGAOR, 61st Session, Supp No 49, UN Doc A/RES/61/295 (2007).

48 *Ibid*, art 25.

49 *Ibid*, art 24.

50 *Ibid*, art 32(1).

51 *Report of the Special Rapporteur on the Rights of Indigenous Peoples, James Anaya – Extractive Industries and Indigenous peoples*, OHCHR, 24th Session, UN Doc A/HRC/24/41 (2013).

52 See generally Laura Westra, *Environmental Justice and the Rights of Indigenous Peoples* (Oxford: Routledge, 2013).

53 See Ciaran O'Faircheallaigh, "Extractive Industries and Indigenous Peoples: A Changing Dynamic?" (2013) 30 J Rural Stud 20 at 20.

54 *Report of the Independent Expert on the Issue of Human Rights Obligations Relating to the Enjoyment of a Safe, Clean, Healthy and*

Sustainable Environment, John H Knox: Preliminary Report, OHCHR, 22nd Session, UN Doc A/HRC/22/43 (2012) at para 28.

55 John Borrows, "Earth-Bound: Indigenous Law and Environmental Reconciliation" in Michael Asch, John Borrows and James Tully, eds, *Resurgence and Reconciliation: Indigenous-Settler Relations and Earth Teachings* (Toronto: University of Toronto Press, 2018) at 49–50 [Borrows, "Earth-Bound"]; Richardson, *supra* note 46.

56 See e.g. Richardson, *supra* note 46.

57 See e.g. *Case of the Indigenous Communities of the Lhaka Honhat Association (Our Land) v Argentina* (2020) Inter-Am Ct HR (Ser C) No 400; John Borrows, "Living between Water and Rocks: First Nations, Environmental Planning, and Democracy" (1997) 47:4 UTLJ 417 [Borrows, "Living between Rocks and Water"].

58 James SY Henderson, "Empowering Treaty Federalism" (1994) 58:2 Sask L Rev 241 at 242; Westra, *supra* note 52 at 126.

59 Gordon Christie, "A Colonial Reading of Recent Jurisprudence: *Sparrow, Delgamuukw, and Haida Nation*" (2005) 23 Windsor YB Access Just 17 at 50.

60 Richardson, *supra* note 46; Borrows, "Earth-Bound", *supra* note 40 at 49–50.

61 See e.g. Stephen T Garnett et al., "A Spatial Overview of the Global Importance of Indigenous Lands for Conservation" (2018) 1:7 Nat Sustain 369; Allen Blackman et al., "Titling Indigenous Communities Protects Forests in the Peruvian Amazon" (2017) 114:16 Proc Natl Acad Sci USA 4123.

62 Borrows, "Living between Rocks and Water", *supra* note 57 at 425.

63 See e.g. Rebecca Tsosie, "Climate Change, Sustainability, and Globalization: Charting the Future of Indigenous Environmental Self-Determination" (2009) 4:2 Envtl Energy L Pol'y J 188; Theresa A McClenaghan, "Why Should Aboriginal Peoples Exercise Governance over Environmental Issues?" (2002) 51 UNBLJ 211; Winona LaDuke, "Traditional Ecological Knowledge and Environmental Futures" (1994) 5:1 Colo J Intl Envtl L Pol'y 127.

64 See Craig Kauffman, "Managing People for the Benefit of the Land: Practising Earth Jurisprudence in Te Urewera, New Zealand" (2020) 27:3 ISLE 578.

65 See Craig M Kauffman and Pamela L Martin, "Can Rights of Nature Make Development More Sustainable? Why Some Ecuadorian Cases Succeed and Others Fail" (2017) 92 World Dev 130.

66 See Elizabeth MacPherson et al., "Constitutional Law, Ecosystems and Indigenous Peoples in Colombia: Biocultural Rights and Legal Subjects" (2020) 9:3 Transnat'l Envtl Law 1.

67 *Center for Social Justice Studies et al v Presidency of the Republic et al* [2016], Constitutional Court of Colombia 622/16 at para 5.11.

68 Klaus Bosselmann, "Ecological Justice and Law" in Benjamin J Richardson and Stepan Wood, eds, *Environmental Law for Sustainability: A Reader* (Oxford: Hart Publishing, 2006) 129 at 163; Ecological Law and Governance Association, "Siena Declaration" (October 2017), online: *ELGA* <https://elgaworld.org/siena-declaration>.

69 See Boyd, "The Environmental Rights Revolution", *supra* note 3 at 63–66.
70 Gerd Winter, "Ecological Proportionality: An Emerging Principle of Law for Nature?" in Christina Voigt, ed., *A Rule of Law for Nature: New Dimensions and Ideas in Environmental Law* (Cambridge: Cambridge University Press: 2013) 111 at 129. See also Hana Mükkerivá, "Right to Environment, Balancing of Competing Interests and Proportionality" (2018) 2:8 Lawyer Q 129.
71 See e.g. Ashish Kothari et al., *Pluriverse: A Post-Development Dictionary* (New Delhi: Tulika Books, 2019).
72 See e.g. Eric R Potyondy "Sustaining the Unsustainable: Development of the Denver Basin Aquifers" (2005) 9:1 U Denv Water L Rev 121.
73 See e.g. Borrows, "Earth-Bound", *supra* note 55.
74 See generally David Grinlinton and Prue Taylor, *Property Rights and Sustainability: The Evolution of Property Rights to Meet Ecological Challenges* (Leiden: Brill, 2011); Eric T Freyfogle, "Ethics, Community, and Private Land" (1996) 23:4 Ecology LQ 631.
75 See Klaus Bosselmann, "Property Rights and Sustainability: Can They Be Reconciled?" in David Grinlinton and Prue Taylor, eds, *Property Rights and Sustainability: The Evolution of Property Rights to Meet Ecological Challenges* (Leiden: Brill, 2011) 21 at 42.
76 See e.g. Peter D Burdon, *Earth Jurisprudence: Private Property and the Environment*, 1st ed. (Abingdon: Routledge, 2015).
77 [cite].
78 Boyd, "The Environmental Rights Revolution", *supra* note 3 at 68.
79 *Constitution of Romania* (8 December 1991) at art 44, para 7.
80 *Constitution of the Plurinational State of Bolivia* (7 February 2009) at art 56.
81 Bosselmann, *supra* note 75 at 38–39.
82 *Ibid* at 42.

References

Anaya, S James, *Indigenous Peoples in International Law*, 2nd ed. (New York: Oxford University Press, 2004).
Blackman, Allen et al., "Titling Indigenous Communities Protects Forests in the Peruvian Amazon" (2017) 114:16 *Proceedings of the National Academy of Sciences of the United States of America* 4123.
Borrows, John, "Earth-Bound: Indigenous Law and Environmental Reconciliation" in Michael Asch, John Borrows and James Tully, eds, *Resurgence and Reconciliation: Indigenous-Settler Relations and Earth Teachings* (Toronto: University of Toronto Press, 2018) 49.
Borrows, John, "Living between Water and Rocks: First Nations, Environmental Planning, and Democracy" (1997) 47:4 UTLJ 417.
Bosselmann, Klaus, "Ecological Justice and Law" in Benjamin J Richardson & Stepan Wood, *Environmental Law for Sustainability: A Reader* (Oxford: Hart Publishing, 2006) 129.

Bosselmann, Klaus, "Property Rights and Sustainability: Can They Be Reconciled?" in David Grinlinton & Prue Taylor, eds, *Property Rights and Sustainability: The Evolution of Property Rights to Meet Ecological Challenges* (Leiden: Brill, 2011) 21.

Boyd, David R, *The Environmental Rights Revolution: A Global Study of Constitutions, Human Rights, and the Environment* (Vancouver: University of British Columbia Press, 2012).

Boyd, David R, *The Right to a Healthy Environment: Revitalizing Canada's Constitution* (Vancouver: UBC Press, 2015).

Burdon, Peter D, *Earth Jurisprudence: Private Property and the Environment*, 1st ed. (Abingdon, Oxon: Routledge, 2015).

Case of the Indigenous Communities of the Lhaka Honhat Association (Our Land) v Argentina (2020) Inter-Am Ct HR (Ser C) No 400.

Center for Social Justice Studies et al v Presidency of the Republic et al [2016], Constitutional Court of Colombia 622/16.

Christie, Gordon C, "A Colonial Reading of Recent Jurisprudence: *Sparrow, Delgamuukw, and Haida Nation*" (2005) 23 Windsor YB Access Just 17.

Collins, Lynda M, "An Ecologically Literate Reading of the *Canadian Charter of Rights and Freedoms*" (2009) 26:1 Windsor Rev Legal Soc Issues 7.

Collins, Lynda M, "Are We There Yet? The Right to Environment in International and European Law" (2007) 3:2 JSDLP 119.

Collins, Lynda M, "The United Nations, Human Rights and the Environment" in Louis J Kotzé & Anna Grear, eds, *Research Handbook on Human Rights and the Environment* (London: Edward Elgar, 2015) 219 at 244.

Collins, Lynda M & David Boyd, "Non-Regression and the *Charter* Right to a Healthy Environment" (2016) 29 J Envtl L Prac 285 at 292.

Constitution of Albania (26 October 2012).

Constitution of Ecuador (10 August 2008).

Constitution of Romania (8 December 1991).

Constitution of the Czech Republic (16 December 1992).

Constitution of the Democratic Republic of Timor-Leste (20 May 2002).

Constitution of the Dominican Republic (13 June 2015).

Constitution of the Plurinational State of Bolivia (7 February 2009).

Constitution of the Republic of Chad (4 May 2018).

Cuadros, Gregorio M, "Environmental Rights, Responsibility and Care: A New Constitutional Paradigm" in Jordi Jaria-Manzano & Susana Borrás, eds, *Research Handbook on Climate Constitutionalism* (London: Edward Elgar, 2019) 176.

Dworkin, Ronald, *Taking Rights Seriously* (Cambridge: Harvard University Press, 1977).

Ebeku, Kaniye SA, "Constitutional Right to a Healthy Environment and Human Rights Approaches to Environmental Protection in Nigeria: *Gbemre v. Shell* Revisited" (2008) 16:3 RECIEL 312.

Ecological Law and Governance Association, "Siena Declaration" (October 2017), online: *ELGA* <https://elgaworld.org/siena-declaration>.

Freyfogle, Eric T, "Ethics, Community, and Private Land" (1996) 23:4 Ecol LQ 631.

Garnett, Stephen T et al., "A Spatial Overview of the Global Importance of Indigenous Lands for Conservation" (2018) 1:7 Nat Sustain 369.

Garver, Geoffrey, *Ecological Law and the Planetary Crisis: A Legal Guide for Harmony on Earth* (London: Routledge, 2020).

Gbemre v Shell Petroleum Development Co Nigeria Ltd, [2005] FHC/B/CS/53/05 (Nigeria).

Gellers, Joshua C & Chris Jeffords, "Towards Environmental Democracy? Procedural Environmental Rights and Environmental Justice" (2018) 18 Global Envtl Polit 99.

Grear, Anna, "Human Rights and New Horizons: Thoughts toward a New Juridical Ontology" (2017) 43:1 Sci Technol Hum Values 129.

Grinlinton, David & Prue Taylor, *Property Rights and Sustainability: The Evolution of Property Rights to Meet Ecological Challenges* (Leiden: Brill, 2011).

Henderson, James SY, "Empowering Treaty Federalism" (1994) 58:2 Sask L Rev 241.

Indian Council for Enviro-Legal Action v Union of India, [1996] 5 Supreme Court Cases 281 (India).

Jeffords, Chris & Joshua C Gellers, "Constitutionalizing Environmental Rights: A Practical Guide" (2017) 9:1 J Hum Rts Prac 136.

Jeffords, Christopher, "On the Temporal Effects of Static Constitutional Environmental Rights Provisions on Access to Improved Sanitation Facilities and Water Sources" (2016) 7:1 J Hum Rts Envtl 74.

Kauffman, Craig, "Managing People for the Benefit of the Land: Practising Earth Jurisprudence in Te Urewera, New Zealand" (2020) 27:3 ISLE 578.

Kauffman, Craig M & Pamela L Martin, "Can Rights of Nature Make Development More Sustainable? Why Some Ecuadorian Cases Succeed and Others Fail" (2017) 92 World Dev 130.

Knox, John H, "Human Rights, Environmental Protection and the Sustainable Development Goals" (2015) 24 Wash Intl L J 517.

Kothari, Ashish et al., *Pluriverse: A Post-Development Dictionary* (New Delhi: Tulika Books, 2019).

Kotzé, Louis J, "Human Rights and the Environment in the Anthropocene" (2014) 1:3 Anthropocene Rev 252.

Kotzé, Louis J & Paola V Calzadilla, "Somewhere between Rhetoric and Reality: Environmental Constitutionalism and the Rights of Nature in Ecuador" (2017) 6:3 Transnat'l Envtl Law 401.

LaDuke, Winona, "Traditional Ecological Knowledge and Environmental Futures" (1994) 5:1 Colo J Intl Envtl L Pol'y 127.

Lee, John, "The Underlying Legal Theory to Support a Well-Defined Human Right to a Healthy Environment as a Principle of Customary International Law" (2000) 25 Colum J Envtl L 238.

MacLean, Jason, "You Say You Want an Environmental Rights Revolution: Try Changing Canadians Minds Instead (of the *Charter*)" (2018) 49:1 Ottawa L Rev 185.

MacPherson, Elizabeth et al., "Constitutional Law, Ecosystems and Indigenous Peoples in Colombia: Biocultural Rights and Legal Subjects" (2020) 9:3 Transnat'l Envtl L 1.

May, James R, "The Case for Environmental Human Rights: Recognition, Implementation and Outcomes" (2021) Cardozo L Rev (forthcoming).

May, James R & Erin Daly, *Global Environmental Constitutionalism* (Cambridge: Cambridge University Press, 2014).

McClenaghan, Theresa A, "Why Should Aboriginal Peoples Exercise Governance over Environmental Issues?" (2002) 51 UNBLJ 211.

MC Mehta v India, [1985] WP (Civil) No 12739 of 1985 (India).

Metcalfe, Cherie, "Indigenous Rights and the Environment: Evolving International Law" (2004) 35:1 Ottawa L Rev 101.

Minors Oposa v Secretary of the Department of Environment and Natural Resources (1993), 33 ILM 173.

Mükkerivá, Hana, "Right to Environment, Balancing of Competing Interests and Proportionality" (2018) 2:8 Lawyer Q 129.

Norbert Brunner et al., "The Human Right to Water in Law and Implementation" (2015) 4:3 Laws 413.

O'Faircheallaigh, Ciaran, "Extractive Industries and Indigenous Peoples: A Changing Dynamic?" (2013) 30 J Rural Stud 20.

Pirjatanniemi, Elina, *Greening Human Rights Law* (London: Routledge, 2016)

Political Constitution of the Republic of Colombia (4 July 1991).

Potyondy, Eric R, "Sustaining the Unsustainable: Development of the Denver Basin Aquifers" (2005) 9:1 U Denv Water L Rev 121.

Razzaque, Jona, *Public Interest Environmental Litigation in India, Pakistan, and Bangladesh* (The Hague: Kluwer Law International, 2004) at 87 *et seq.*

Report of the Independent Expert on the Issue of Human Rights Obligations Relating to the Enjoyment of a Safe, Clean, Healthy and Sustainable Environment, John H. Knox: Compilation of Good Practices, OHCHR, 78th Session, UN Doc A/HRC/28/61 (2015).

Report of the Independent Expert on the Issue of Human Rights Obligations Relating to the Enjoyment of a Safe, Clean, Healthy and Sustainable Environment, John H Knox: Preliminary Report, OHCHR, 22nd Session, UN Doc A/HRC/22/43 (2012).

Report of the Special Rapporteur on the Issue of Human Rights Obligations in Relation to the Enjoyment of a Safe, Clean, Healthy and Sustainable Environment: Human Rights Depend on a Healthy Biosphere, OHCHR, 75th Session, UN Doc A/75/161 (2020).

Report of the Special Rapporteur on the Issue of Human Rights Obligations Relating to the Enjoyment of a Safe, Clean, Healthy and Sustainable

Environment: Right to a Healthy Environment: Good Practices, OHCHR, 43rd Session, UN Doc A/HRC/43/53 (2020).

Report of the Special Rapporteur on the Issue of Human Rights Obligations Relating to the Enjoyment of a Safe, Clean, Healthy and Sustainable Environment: Safe Climate, OHCHR, 73rd Session, UN Doc A/73/188 (2018).

Report of the Special Rapporteur on the Rights of Indigenous Peoples, James Anaya – Extractive Industries and Indigenous peoples, OHCHR, 24th Session, UN Doc A/HRC/24/41 (2013).

Requested by the Republic of Colombia: The Environment and Human Rights (2017), Advisory Opinion OC-23/17, Inter-Am Ct HR (Ser A) No 23.

Richardson, Benjamin J, "The Ties that Bind: Indigenous Peoples and Environmental Governance" in Benjamin J Richardson, Shin Imai & Kent McNeil, eds, *Indigenous Peoples and the Law: Comparative and Critical Perspectives* (Oxford: Hart Publishing, 2009) 337.

Shelton, Dinah, *Human Rights and the Environment* (Cheltenham: Edward Elgar Publishing, 2011).

Shelton, Dinah & Donald K Anton, *Environmental Protection and Human Rights* (Cambridge: Cambridge University Press, 2011).

Subhash Kumar v State of Bihar et al, [1991] AIR 420, 1991 SCR (1) 5 (India). WP (Civil) No 381 of 1988, D/-9-1-91 (Supreme Court of India).

Tsosie, Rebecca, "Climate Change, Sustainability, and Globalization: Charting the Future of Indigenous Environmental Self-Determination" (2009) 4:2 Envtl Energy L Pol'y J 188.

United Nations Declaration on the Rights of Indigenous Peoples, GA Res 295, UNGAOR, 61st Session, Supp No 49, UN Doc A/RES/61/295 (2007).

Westra, Laura, *Environmental Justice and the Rights of Indigenous Peoples* (Oxford: Routledge, 2013).

Winter, Gerd, "Ecological Proportionality: An Emerging Principle of Law for Nature?" in Christina Voigt, ed., *A Rule of Law for Nature: New Dimensions and Ideas in Environmental Law* (Cambridge: Cambridge University Press: 2013) 111 at 129.

Zia v WAPDA, [1994] PLD SC 693 (Pakistan).

4 Intergenerational equity and the public trust doctrine

An ecological approach to constitutionalism requires the recognition of a few basic realities: "that individuals are *not* separate from their environment, entitlements are *not* separate from responsibilities, the private is *not* separate from the public, the local is *not* separate from the global [and] the present is *not* separate from the future...".[1] The doctrines of intergenerational equity and the public trust discussed in this chapter offer two avenues for incorporating the intertemporal and collective dimensions of ecological law into constitutions. Although both doctrines are essentially anthropocentric, they undoubtedly hold the potential to improve the sustainability of ecosystems (and the ecosphere as a whole) with manifold benefits to the nonhuman living world.

The recognition of kinship with, and an obligation towards, future generations is consonant with a wide range of legal and philosophical traditions. Islamic law, for example, posits Muslims as trustees (or stewards) of the natural world with duties towards both current and future generations.[2] Several Asian philosophical and religious traditions also include notions of responsibility to future generations,[3] which in some cases are thought to include reincarnations of those currently living.[4] Streams of African customary law recognise ownership/stewardship of land by the collective, including future generations. One Ghanaian chief has explained that in this conceptualisation, "land belongs to a vast family of whom many are dead, a few are living, and a countless host are still unborn".[5] Similarly, in what is now known as North America, Haudenosaunee law explicitly requires decisionmakers to take into account impacts extending seven generations into the future.[6] Thus, intergenerational equity resonates with diverse streams of legal thought, including contemporary articulations of ecological law.

Scope and content of the doctrine of
intergenerational equity

The doctrine of intergenerational equity[7] is a comprehensive legal framework for environmental governance most fully developed by Professor Edith Brown Weiss in her 1989 book, *In Fairness to Future Generations*.[8] Brown Weiss posits the present generation of humans as both beneficiaries of a planetary legacy passed down from the past and trustees of the planetary legacy for future generations.[9] The doctrine recognises both the rights of the present generation to use and enjoy ecological resources and its obligation to adequately conserve such resources for the future.[10] It validates both the interest of the individual in an adequate quality of life and the value of the intertemporal world community in which every individual is situated. The constitutional inclusion of intergenerational equity could play an important role in counteracting political short-termism, which has been viewed as a fundamental challenge to sustainability in democratic societies: "The need to appease the electorate in regular five year or similar intervals means that politicians direct their actions according to the needs and desires of the present citizens".[11]

While it is clearly related to dominant definitions of sustainable development, the doctrine of intergenerational equity is far more robust and detailed and, thus, capable of providing clear constitutional guidance. Brown Weiss identifies three core constituents of intergenerational equity: "Conservation of Options" requires the present generation to conserve the diversity of the natural and cultural resource base.[12] The second principle, "Conservation of Quality", requires the present generation to pass the planet (or the nation) on to future generations "in no worse condition than that in which it was received".[13] The third principle, "Conservation of Access", requires that members of the present generation be provided with equitable rights of access to our ecological legacy, while conserving this access for future generations. Brown Weiss argues that this principle requires privileged members of the present generation to assist the more vulnerable members in both carrying out their conservation obligations and enjoying their rights to benefit from the planetary legacy.[14]

Clarifying these obligations further, Brown Weiss posits that the three planetary obligations translate into specific duties of use. First, the duty to conserve resources requires present generations to conserve both renewable and non-renewable natural resources.[15]

Second, the duty to ensure equitable use, defined as "reasonable, non-discriminatory access to the [planetary] legacy",[16] includes both the negative obligation to refrain from infringing on the access rights of other beneficiaries and positive obligations to "assist those who would otherwise be too poor to have reasonable access and use".[17]

The third duty, the duty to avoid adverse impacts on the environment, flows from responsibilities both to present co-beneficiaries of the planetary trust and future generations.[18] It "emphasises prevention and mitigation of damage"[19] and includes procedural environmental rights and duties including notice, information, consultation and environmental assessment.[20] With respect to environmental assessment in particular, Brown Weiss observes that intergenerational equity requires adequate consideration of long-term impacts.[21] The fourth duty is to prevent disasters, minimise damage and provide emergency assistance, and the fifth is to compensate for damage to the environment.[22]

Planetary (or ecological) rights in the doctrine of intergenerational equity include the right to diversity, quality and access. Rights in this context have a dual nature. The planetary rights of future generations are group rights, not individual rights (and should be asserted by a representative of the group as a whole),[23] but crystallise into individual rights within the present generation.

Intergenerational equity in national constitutions

More than 30 domestic constitutions reference the environmental needs, rights or interests of "future generations" explicitly.[24] For example, Algeria's draft 2020 constitution provides that "The State shall ensure the rational usage and preservation of water for future generations",[25] and Brazil's constitution provides that "[t]he Government and the community have a duty to defend and to preserve the environment for present and future generations".[26] Several constitutions make multiple environmental references to future generations. For example, the constitution of Bolivia declares the environmental welfare of future generations as an "essential purpose and function of the state",[27] provides that the "right to a healthy, protected, and balanced environment ... must be granted to individuals and collectives of present and future generations ..."[28] and imposes a duty on all Bolivians to "protect and defend the natural resources, and to contribute to their sustainable use in order to preserve the rights of future generations".[29]

Hungary's constitution also references the interests of future generations multiple times and establishes a Commission for Fundamental Rights whose members "shall [among other things] protect the interests of future generations...".[30] Tunisia's 2014 constitution similarly constitutionalises governance for the future, establishing a Sustainable Development and Rights of Future Generations Commission which "shall be consulted on draft laws related to economic, social and environmental issues, as well as development plans".[31]

Case law

Several constitutional judgements from courts around the world have recognised the doctrine of intergenerational equity and/or the environmental rights and interests of future generations. In the famous 1993 judgment in *Minors Oposa*, for example, the Supreme Court of the Philippines granted standing to minors to represent their own environmental rights and those of future generations.[32] This decision influenced the cancellation of a majority of timber harvesting licenses and reduction in deforestation over the ensuing years.[33]

Fifteen years after *Oposa*, the Philippine Supreme Court followed up with one of the most detailed and ambitious environmental rulings in world history, ordering an intensive and comprehensive clean-up of Manila Bay.[34] The Court retained a continuing *mandamus* jurisdiction to ensure that the relevant government agencies would faithfully carry out its order. It concluded that such agencies could not "escape their obligation to future generations of Filipinos to keep the waters of the Manila Bay as clean and clear as humanly possible. Anything less would be a betrayal of the trust reposed in them".[35]

In 2014, the Supreme Court of Canada applied a version of intergenerational equity in a case clarifying the nature of Indigenous land rights under section 35 of the Canadian constitution. In *Tsilhqot'in Nation v British Columbia*, the Court held that "incursions on [Indigenous] title cannot be justified if they would substantially deprive future generations of the benefit of the land"[36] and further that Indigenous title lands cannot be put to uses that would "destroy the ability of the land to sustain future generations of [Indigenous] peoples".[37] The Court's reasoning was influenced by its commitment to respect Indigenous legal perspectives in adjudicating claims under section 35.[38] While the notion of ecological obligation to future generations had no precedent in Canadian constitutional law, it is a part of many Indigenous legal systems in the territory now known as Canada.[39]

More recently, the Colombian Supreme Court imposed obligations on the government to reduce deforestation and take other climate measures to respect both environmental human rights and rights of nature, and explicitly recognised a violation of the rights and interests of future generations:

> In terms of intergenerational equity, the transgression is obvious, as the forecast of temperature increase is 1.6 degrees in 2041 and 2.14 in 2071; future generations, including children who brought this action, will be directly affected, unless we presently reduce the deforestation rate to zero.[40]

Several of the ongoing climate cases discussed in Chapter 7 are based in part on arguments for intergenerational equity and the government's duty as trustee of the atmosphere as a climate commons.[41]

The public trust doctrine in constitutional theory and practice

The public trust doctrine provides that natural resources are held in trust by government for the benefit of the present and future citizens and thus cannot be alienated or depleted to an extent that would undermine their long-term viability.[42] The public trust doctrine may be viewed as a domestic mechanism for instantiating the deeper and more detailed doctrine of intergenerational equity discussed above.[43] In the West, the public trust doctrine is thought to derive from Roman law under Justinian: "By the law of nature these things are common to mankind – the air, running water, the sea...".[44] The French *Civil Code* has historically recognised public ownership in navigable rivers, streams, beaches, ports and harbours,[45] and the doctrine also survived into early English Common Law.[46] The Indian Supreme Court has recognised the public trust doctrine as consistent with ancient Indian spiritual teachings and has suggested that it dates back to the Chen dynasty in China.[47]

Constitutionalising the public trust doctrine

Recognition of the public trust concept can be found in a number of national and subnational constitutions. For example, the constitution of the US state of Pennsylvania provides that:

> The people have a right to clean air, pure water, and to the preservation of the natural, scenic, historic, and esthetic values of

the environment. Pennsylvania's public natural resources are the common property of all the people, including generations yet to come. As trustee of these resources, the Commonwealth shall conserve and maintain them for the benefit of all the people.[48]

Since the pivotal 1892 US Supreme Court decision in *Illinois Central Railroad Company v. Illinois*,[49] judges in multiple countries around the world have used the public trust doctrine to protect vital natural resources against government misuse or inaction.[50] In *Illinois*, the Court held that the State could not alienate lakebed property to a private entity because it held title to these submerged lands "in trust for the people of the State that they may enjoy the navigation of the waters, carry on commerce over them, and have liberty of fishing therein freed from the obstruction or interference of private parties".[51] In the majority of American states, the public trust doctrine is limited to protecting navigable waters, shorelines and submerged lands but some have extended the doctrine to protect non-navigable waters, parklands and wildlife and to prevent hazardous pollution.[52] Babcock notes that American courts

> have vigorously used the public trust doctrine to protect communal resources from inconsistent uses and have strictly scrutinized transfers of public trust resources to ensure that the transfers are in the public interest. Courts never lose their power to revoke a transfer that they later find is not in the public interest.[53]

Given that the United States constitutionally protects the right to hold private property, it is remarkable that the public trust doctrine has been held to supersede vested property interests in the United States.[54]

In India, the Supreme Court first recognised the public trust doctrine in the 1997 case of *Mehta v Nath*.[55] In *Nath*, a private developer with ties to the Minister for Environment and Forests had been granted licenses to land encroaching on a public forest and had diverted a streambed in order to protect its property from flooding. The Indian Supreme Court adopted the public trust doctrine (citing English common law, relevant US jurisprudence and Indian spiritual traditions) and used it to invalidate the leases and order ecological restoration to repair the damage resulting from the developer's activities. The Court subsequently situated the public trust doctrine within India's constitutional right to life and applied it to cases involving the construction and operation of an underground shopping centre in a public park[56] and the exploitation of natural gas deposits in Indian waters.[57]

In Kenya, judicial leadership appears to have led to explicit constitutional recognition of the public trust doctrine. In its 2006 decision in *Waweru v Republic [of Kenya]*, a criminal case arising from the discharge of raw sewage into the Kiserian River, the High Court of Kenya recognised an implicit environmental right within Kenya's constitutional right to life. It further held that this environmental right included the public trust doctrine: "In the case of land resources, forests, wetlands and waterways ... the Government and its agencies are under a public trust to manage them in a way that maintains a proper balance between the economic benefits of development with the needs of a clean environment".[58] Furthermore, "the water table and the river courses affected are held in trust by the present generation for the future generations".[59]

In fashioning an appropriate remedy, the Court declared that "the government itself is both under ... statutory obligation[s] ... and also under a public trust to provide adequate land for the establishment of treatment works" and issued an order in the nature of *mandamus* compelling the government to construct sewage treatment facilities.[60] Only a few years after the decision in *Waweru*, Kenya's 2010 Constitution explicitly incorporated public trust concepts in a number of its provisions. The new right to a healthy environment under Article 42, for example, includes the right the right "to have the environment protected for the benefit of present and future generations through legislative and other measures...".[61] Article 61 provides that "[a]ll land in Kenya belongs to the people collectively as a nation, as communities and as individuals".[62] Article 69 requires the State to "ensure sustainable exploitation, utilisation, management and conservation of the environment and natural resources, and ensure the equitable sharing of the accruing benefits".[63]

The *Manila Bay* and *Tsilhqot'in* cases discussed above can also be understood as reflecting the public trust doctrine, though in the latter the Supreme Court of Canada imposes a kind of public trust on Indigenous peoples but not on the State itself.

Limitations

From an ecological law perspective, the obvious weakness in both the public trust doctrine and the doctrine of intergenerational equity is their anthropocentrism. With the possible exception of Bolivia's intergenerational and holistic environmental right, most articulations of the public trust and intergenerational equity canvassed here fail all three of Sbert's ecological law criteria. Bosselmann's concept of "ecological justice" would remedy this defect by adding interspecies equity to inter- and intra-generational equity.[64] Another approach would be to complement intergenerational environmental rights and duties with a recognition of the inherent personhood or rights of nature, as discussed in Chapter 5.

Notes

1 Klaus Bosselmann, "Property Rights and Sustainability: Can They Be Reconciled?" in David Grinlinton and Prue Taylor, eds, *Property Rights and Sustainability: The Evolution of Property Rights to Meet Ecological Challenges* (Leiden: Martinus Nijhoff, 2011) 21 at 34.
2 Azim Nanji, "The Right to Development: Social and Cultural Rights and Duties to the Community" in *Proceedings of the Seminar on Islamic Perspectives on the Universal Declaration of Human Rights*, UN Doc. HR/IP/SEM/1999/1 (PART II Sec. 2), (1999) at 346 (citing Quranic ayah 2:30).
3 Edith B Weiss, *In Fairness to Future Generations: International Law, Common Patrimony, and Intergenerational Equity* (Tokyo: UN University Press, 1989) at 20 [Weiss, *In Fairness*].
4 See e.g. John M Peek, "Buddhism, Human Rights, and the Japanese State" (1995) 17:3 Hum Rts Q 527 at 529.
5 Weiss, *In Fairness, supra* note 3.
6 *The Great Law of Peace of the Longhouse People (Iroquois League of Six Nations)* Chapter 28 (White Roots of Peace, Mohawk Nation at Akwesasne, Rooseveltown, NY 1973).
7 Lynda M Collins, "Revisiting the Doctrine of Intergenerational Equity in Global Environmental Governance" (2007) 30:1 Dal LJ 79.
8 Weiss, *In Fairness, supra* note 3.
9 *Ibid* at 20.
10 *Ibid.*
11 Jörg C Tremmel and Martin Viehöver, "The Dilemma of Short-Term Politics" (2002) 3 Gener Justice! 12 at 12.
12 Weiss, *In Fairness, supra* note 3 at 41.
13 Edith B Weiss, "Our Rights and Obligations to Future Generations for the Environment" (1990) 84 AJIL 198 at 202.
14 Weiss, *In Fairness, supra* note 3 at 45.
15 *Ibid* at 50.
16 *Ibid* at 55.
17 *Ibid.*
18 *Ibid* at 59–60.
19 *Ibid* at 60.
20 *Ibid* at 60–61.
21 *Ibid* at 63.
22 *Ibid* at 50–70.
23 *Ibid* at 96.
24 David R Boyd, *The Environmental Rights Revolution: A Global Study of Constitutions, Human Rights, and the Environment* (Vancouver: UBC Press, 2012) at 70 [Boyd, *Environmental Rights Revolution*]; James R

May and Erin Daly, "Six Trends in Global Environmental Constitutionalism" (2018) Environmental Constitutionalism: Impact on Legal Systems? (forthcoming). https://papers.ssrn.com/sol3/papers.cfm?abstract_id=3252636.

25 *Constitution of Algeria* (1989, reinstated in 1996 with amendments through 2016) at art 64.

26 *Constitution of the Federative Republic of Brazil* (5 October 1988, with Amendments from 1992 to 2010) at art 225.

27 *Constitution of 2009 of the Plurinational State of Bolivia* (9 February 2009) at art 9(6).

28 *Ibid* at art 33.

29 *Ibid* at art 108 (15).

30 *Constitution of Hungary* (2011) at art 30(3).

31 *Constitution of Tunisia* (26 January 2014) at art 129.

32 *Minors Oposa v Secretary of the Department of Environment and Natural Resources* (1993), 33 ILM 173 (1994) (Philippines).

33 Boyd, *Environmental Rights Revolution, supra* note 24 at 167.

34 *Metropolitan Manila Bay Development Authority v Concerned Residents of Manila Bay* (2011), GR Nos 171947-48 (Supreme Court of the Philippines) [*Metropolitan Development v Residents of Manila*]; Boyd, *Environmental Rights Revolution, supra* note 24 at 168–9.

35 *Metropolitan Development v Residents of Manila, supra* note 34; Boyd, *Environmental Rights Revolution, supra* note 24 at 168–9.

36 *Tsilhqot'in Nation v British Columbia*, 2014 SCC 44 at para 86.

37 *Ibid* at para 121.

38 *Delgamuukw v British Columbia*, [1997] 3 SCR 1010 at paras 84–87, 153 DLR (4th) 193; see James (Sákéj) Youngblood Henderson et al., *Aboriginal Tenure in the Constitution of Canada* (Toronto: Carswell, 2000) at 8.

39 See generally John Borrows, *Canada's Indigenous Constitution* (Toronto: University of Toronto Press, 2010).

40 Corte Suprema de Justicia [Supreme Court of Justice], Bogotá, 5 April 2018, *Luis Armando Tolosa Villabona, STC4360-2018*, Radicación no. 11001-22-03-000-2018-00319-01 (Columbia) at para 11.2; see also Lydia Slobodian, "Defending the Future: Intergenerational Equity in Climate Litigation" (2020) 32:3 Geo Envtl L Rev 569.

41 See e.g. Zachary L Berliner, "What about Uncle Sam? Carving a New Place for the Public Trust Doctrine in Federal Climate Litigation" (2018) 21 U Pa J L Soc Change 339; Kassandra Castillo, "Climate Change & The Public Trust Doctrine: An Analysis of Atmospheric Trust Litigatin" (2015) 6 San Diego J Clim Energy L 221.

42 See generally Michael C Blumm and Mary Wood, *The Public Trust Doctrine in Environmental and Natural Resources Law*, 3rd ed. (Durham, NC: Carolina Academic Press, 2021).

43 Weiss, *In Fairness, supra* note 3.

44 Thomas Sandars, *The Institutes of Justinian* (London: Woodfall and Kinder, 1853) at 176.

45 *British Columbia v Canadian Forest Products Ltd*, 2004 SCC 38 at para 75.

46 *Bracton on the Laws and Customs of England*, vol. 2, translated by Samuel E Thorne (Cambridge, MA: Harvard University Press, 1968) at 39–40.

47 *Reliance Natural Resources Ltd v Reliance Industries Ltd*, [2010] INSC 374 (Supreme Court of India) at para 98 [*Reliance*].

48 *Constitution of the Commonwealth of Pennsylvania* (18 May 1971) at art 1, s 27.

49 *Illinois Central R Co v Illinois*, 146 US 387 (Supreme Court of the United States, 1892) [*Illinois*].

50 Michael C Blumm and Rachel D Guthrie, "Internationalizing the Public Trust Doctrine: Natural Law and Constitutional and Statutory Approaches to Fulfilling the Saxion Vision" (2012) 45 UC Davis L Rev 741.

51 *Illinois*, *supra* note 49 at 452.

52 Alexandra B Klass, "The Public Trust Doctrine in the Shadow of State Environmental Rights Laws: A Case Study" (2015) 45:2 Envtl L 431 at 438–9. See generally Blumm and Wood, *supra* note 42; Mary Christina Wood, *Nature's Trust: Environmental Law for a New Ecological Age* (Cambridge: Cambridge University Press, 2013).

53 Hope M Babcock, "The Public Trust Doctrine: What a Tall Tale They Tell" (2009) 61:2 SCL Rev 393 at 397 (internal citations omitted).

54 *Ibid.*

55 *Mehta v Nath* (1997), 1 SCC 388 (India). See also Paul A Barresi, "Mobilizing the Public Trust Doctrine in Support of Publicly Owned Forests as Carbon Dioxide Sinks in India and the United States" (2012) 23:1 Colo J Int'l Envtl L Pol'y 39 at 56–57.

56 *MI Builders Pvt Ltd v Sahu*, AIR 1999 SC 2468 (Supreme Court of India).

57 *Reliance*, *supra* note 47.

58 *Waweru v Republic* (2006), Misc Civil Application No 118 of 2004 (High Court of Kenya) at para 42.

59 *Ibid* at para 48.

60 *Ibid* at para 52.

61 *Constitution of Kenya* (7 April 2010) at art 42(a).

62 *Ibid* at art 61(1).

63 *Ibid* at art 69(1)(a).

64 Klaus Bosselmann, "Ecological Justice and Law" in Benjamin J Richardson and Stepan Wood, *Environmental Law for Sustainability: A Reader* (Oxford: Hart Publishing, 2006) 129.

References

Babcock, Hope M, "The Public Trust Doctrine: What a Tall Tale They Tell" (2009) 61:2 SCL Rev 393.

Barresi, Paul A, "Mobilizing the Public Trust Doctrine in Support of Publicly Owned Forests as Carbon Dioxide Sinks in India and the United States" (2012) 23:1 Colo J Int'l Envtl L Pol'y 39.

Berliner, Zachary L, "What about Uncle Sam? Carving a New Place for the Public Trust Doctrine in Federal Climate Litigation" (2018) 21 U Pa J L Soc Change 339.

Blumm, Michael C & Rachel D Guthrie, "Internationalizing the Public Trust Doctrine: Natural Law and Constitutional and Statutory Approaches to Fulfilling the Saxion Vision" (2012) 45 UC Davis L Rev 741.

Blumm, Michael C & Mary Wood, *The Public Trust Doctrine in Environmental and Natural Resources Law*, 3rd ed. (Durham, NC: Carolina Academic Press, 2021).

Borrows, John, *Canada's Indigenous Constitution* (Toronto: University of Toronto Press, 2010).

Bosselmann, Klaus, "Ecological Justice and Law" in Benjamin J Richardson & Stepan Wood, *Environmental Law for Sustainability: A Reader* (Oxford: Hart Publishing, 2006) 129.

Bosselmann, Klaus, "Property Rights and Sustainability: Can They Be Reconciled?" in David Grinlinton & Prue Taylor, eds, *Property Rights and Sustainability: The Evolution of Property Rights to Meet Ecological Challenges* (Leiden: Brill, 2011) 21.

Boyd, David R, *The Environmental Rights Revolution: A Global Study of Constitutions, Human Rights, and the Environment* (Vancouver: UBC Press, 2012).

Bracton on the Laws and Customs of England, vol. 2, translated by Samuel E Thorne (Cambridge, MA: Harvard University Press, 1968).

British Columbia v Canadian Forest Products Ltd, 2004 SCC 38.

Castillo, Kassandra, "Climate Change & The Public Trust Doctrine: An Analysis of Atmospheric Trust Litigation" (2015) 6 San Diego J Clim Energy L 221.

Collins, Lynda M, "Revisiting the Doctrine of Intergenerational Equity in Global Environmental Governance" (2007) 30:1 Dal LJ 79.

Constitution of 2009 of the Plurinational State of Bolivia (9 February 2009).

Constitution of Algeria (1989, reinstated in 1996 with amendments through 2016).

Constitution of Hungary (2011).

Constitution of Kenya (7 April 2010).

Constitution of the Commonwealth of Pennsylvania (18 May 1971).

Constitution of the Federative Republic of Brazil (5 October 1988, with Amendments from 1992 to 2010).

Constitution of Tunisia (26 January 2014).

Corte Suprema de Justicia [Supreme Court of Justice], Bogotá, 5 April 2018, *Luis Armando Tolosa Villabona, STC4360-2018*, Radicación no. 11001-22-03-000-2018-00319-01 (Columbia).

Delgamuukw v British Columbia, [1997] 3 SCR 1010, 153 DLR (4th) 193.

Henderson, James (Sákéj) Youngblood et al., *Aboriginal Tenure in the Constitution of Canada* (Toronto: Carswell, 2000).

Illinois Central R Co v Illinois, 146 US 387 (Supreme Court of the United States, 1892).

Klass, Alexandra B, "The Public Trust Doctrine in the Shadow of State Environmental Rights Laws: A Case Study" (2015) 45:2 Envtl L 431.

May, James R & Erin Daly, "Six Trends in Global Environmental Constitutionalism" (2018) Environmental Constitutionalism: Impact on Legal Systems? (forthcoming).

Mehta v Nath, [1997]1 SCC 388 (India).

Metropolitan Manila Bay Development Authority v Concerned Residents of Manila Bay, [2011] GR Nos 171947-48 (Supreme Court of the Philippines).

MI Builders Pvt Ltd v Sahu, [1999] AIR 1999 SC 2468 (Supreme Court of India).

Minors Oposa v Secretary of the Department of Environment and Natural Resources, [1993] 33 ILM 173 (Supreme Court of the Philippines).

Nanji, Azim, "The Right to Development: Social and Cultural Rights and Duties to the Community" in *Proceedings of the Seminar on Islamic Perspectives on the Universal Declaration of Human Rights*, UN Doc. HR/IP/SEM/1999/1 (PART II Sec. 2), (1999) at 346 (citing Quranic ayah 2:30).

Peek, John M, "Buddhism, Human Rights, and the Japanese State" (1995) 17:3 Hum Rts Q 527.

Reliance Natural Resources Ltd v Reliance Industries Ltd, [2010] INSC 374 (Supreme Court of India).

Sandars, Thomas, *The Institutes of Justinian* (London: Woodfall and Kinder, 1853).

Slobodian, Lydia, "Defending the Future: Intergenerational Equity in Climate Litigation" (2020) 32:3 Geo Envtl L Rev 569.

The Great Law of Peace of the Longhouse People (Iroquois League of Six Nations) Chapter 28 (White Roots of Peace, Mohawk Nation at Akwesasne, Rooseveltown, NY 1973).

Tsilhqot'in Nation v British Columbia, 2014 SCC 44.

Tremmel, Jörg C & Martin Viehöver, "The Dilemma of Short-Term Politics" (2002) 3 Gener Justice! 12.

Weiss, Edith B, *In Fairness to Future Generations: International Law, Common Patrimony, and Intergenerational Equity* (Tokyo: UN University Press, 1989).

Wood, Mary C, *Nature's Trust: Environmental Law for a New Ecological Age* (Cambridge: Cambridge University Press, 2013).

5 Rights of nature in the ecological constitution

Of all the ideas discussed in this book, recognition of the legal personhood and rights of natural entities is perhaps most consonant with the hallmarks of ecological law: ecocentrism, ecological primacy and ecological justice.[1] The rights-of-nature movement has been widely hailed as one of the greatest legal transformations in human history – one that has the real potential to fundamentally reorient human societies towards sustainability.[2] Indeed, in his brilliant book on the subject, Boyd describes rights of nature as "a legal revolution that could save the world".[3] Crucially, this legal revolution also has the potential to help decolonise environmental law and create space for Indigenous legal orders to guide ecological decision-making going forward.[4] Though not without its critics,[5] the recognition of rights of nature is arguably at the heart of the ecological constitution.

Philosophical and legal foundations

As Deur et al. have observed, "[t]hat there are certain 'rights of Nature' intrinsic to landscapes and life-forms around the world is a revolutionary assertion, yet an assertion with abundant and venerable precedents".[6] In particular, the idea that human beings have relationships with, and owe obligations to, other natural beings such plants, animals, water, soil and the Earth as a whole is well established in Indigenous legal orders around the world.[7] While there is enormous diversity both within and among Indigenous legal systems and societies, a recognition of the inherent dignity of natural entities and obligations of reciprocity between humans and nonhumans seems to be a common thread in many Indigenous cultural, spiritual and legal teachings.[8]

Indeed, James (Sákéj) Youngblood Henderson has written that "[t]he First Nations' relationships with the land have always defined their identity, their spiritual ecology, and their reality".[9] For her part, legal scholar Leanne Betasamosake Simpson of the Michi Saagiig Nishnaabeg Indigenous nation characterises her people's relationship with nature as a form of internationalism, writing:

> ...[M]y nation is not just composed of Nishnaabeg [people]. It is a series of radiating relationships with plant nations, animal nations, insects, bodies of water, air, soil, and spiritual beings, in addition to the Indigenous nations with whom we share parts of our territory.[10]

In many cases, Indigenous thought seems to have appreciated a crucial biological reality that Western science has only recently begun to perceive: human unity with, and dependence upon, the rest of nature.[11]

Borrows recounts an Indigenous Anishnabe legal story (or case report) in which the deer nation deserts the people in battle:

> The Anishinabe were astonished and asked the deer how the Nation had offended them. The deer spoke sadly: "You have wasted our flesh; you have despoiled our haunts; you have desecrated our bones; you have dishonoured us and yourselves. Without you we can live – but without us you cannot live. We can live with or without you". The Anishinabe then asked how they should make amends; they said their negligence was not motivated by ill will. The Anishinabe asked: "How shall we restore what we have taken and what you have lost?" The Chief Deer answered, "Honour and respect our lives and our beings, in life and in death. Do not waste our flesh. Preserve fields and forests for our homes. Cease doing what offends our spirits. To show commitment to these things and as a remembrance of the anguish you have brought upon us, always leave the tobacco leaf from where you take us. Gifts are important to build our relationships once again". The Anishinabe promised to follow the words of the Chief Deer.[12]

Thus, a growing body of Indigenous legal scholarship suggests that, far from being a commodifiable, right-less "thing", many Indigenous nations recognise nature as an integral part of human community on both the material and spiritual levels. A New Zealand judicial decision concerning river diversions reflects this insight, observing:

> The most damaging effect of [the] diversions on Maori has been on the *wairua* or spirituality of the people. Several of the

witnesses talked about the people "grieving" for the rivers. One
needs to understand the culture of the Whanganui River iwi
[nation] to realise how deeply ingrained the saying *ko au te awa,
ko te awa, ko au* [I am the river, the river is me] is to those who
have connections to the river.... Their spirituality is their "connectedness" to the river. To take away part of the river (like the
water or the river shingle) is to take away part of the iwi. To
desecrate the water is to desecrate the iwi. To pollute the water
is to pollute the people.[13]

Even in non-Indigenous Western thought, the idea of human separation from (and dominion over) the natural world is a relatively
new phenomenon.[14] Although Western modes of thought and practice have justly been blamed for creating the legal, socio-political
and economic structures that are arguably at the root of our global
eco-social crisis, the pre-patriarchal, pre-Christian culture of Europe evinced an intimate understanding of and relationship with
nature.[15] No doubt much of this history has been lost, but even
among canonical Western traditions, a vein of ecological thought,
consistent with rights of nature, is discernible.[16]

As Capra and Mattei explain in *The Ecology of Law*, the last mil-
lennium witnessed an unprecedented move in European culture
away from ecological living and towards socio-political and economic systems that were divorced from the biological bottom line
of being human.[17] The thinking of Descartes, Bacon and Newton
transformed nature from a sacred living being to a machine to be
manipulated and subdued for human ends.[18] The rule of law developed as a mechanism to protect state sovereignty and private
property, leaving little space for ecological or social commons.[19] As
technology developed – and colonialism expanded – exponentially
over time, the extractive Western economy became increasingly
unsustainable and globalised, bringing us to the current state of
affairs.[20] However, ecological thinking was never entirely extin-
guished in the West,[21] and the idea of nature's personhood returned
to Western legal thought with Christopher Stone's pivotal 1972 es-
say "Should trees have standing?"[22]

Rights of nature discourse has now been thoroughly elaborated by
scholars and advocates.[23] In his foundational writing on the subject,
cultural historian Thomas Berry argues for constitutional and judicial
recognition of the following fundamental principles, among others:

1   The natural world on the planet Earth has rights, which come
     with existence. These rights come from the same source from

which humans receive their rights, from the universe that brought them into being.

2 Every component of the Earth community has three rights: the right to be, the right to habitat and the right to fulfil its role in the ever-renewing processes of the Earth community.

3 All rights are specific and limited. Rivers have river rights. Birds have bird rights. Insects have insect rights. Humans have human rights. Difference in rights is qualitative, not quantitative. The rights of an insect would be of no value to a tree or a fish.[24]

These ideas find expression in international initiatives such as the Earth Charter,[25] the UN Harmony with Nature Programme[26] and the Universal Declaration of the Rights of Mother Earth,[27] among others. At the national level, a growing number of countries are "ecologizing" statutes and constitutions to recognise the legal personhood and rights of nature.

Rights of nature in national constitutions

Any discussion of constitutional rights of nature must begin with Ecuador's breakthrough 2008 constitution that made history by recognising the rights of Pacha Mama, or Mother Earth. The constitution of Ecuador dedicates an entire chapter to the Rights of Nature, elaborating their scope and content as follows:

Article 71

Nature, or Pacha Mama, where life is reproduced and occurs, has the right to integral respect for its existence and for the maintenance and regeneration of its life cycles, structure, functions and evolutionary processes.

All persons, communities, peoples and nations can call upon public authorities to enforce the rights of nature. To enforce and interpret these rights, the principles set forth in the Constitution shall be observed, as appropriate.

The State shall give incentives to natural persons and legal entities and to communities to protect nature and to promote respect for all the elements comprising an ecosystem.

Article 72

Nature has the right to be restored. This restoration shall be apart from the obligation of the State and natural persons or legal entities to compensate individuals and communities that depend on affected natural systems.

In those cases of severe or permanent environmental impact, including those caused by the exploitation of nonrenewable natural resources, the State shall establish the most effective mechanisms to achieve the restoration and shall adopt adequate measures to eliminate or mitigate harmful environmental consequences.

Article 73

The State shall apply preventive and restrictive measures on activities that might lead to the extinction of species, the destruction of ecosystems and the permanent alteration of natural cycles.

The introduction of organisms and organic and inorganic material that might definitely alter the nation's genetic assets is forbidden.

Article 74

Persons, communities, peoples, and nations shall have the right to benefit from the environment and the natural wealth enabling them to enjoy the good way of living.

Environmental services shall not be subject to appropriation; their production, delivery, use and development shall be regulated by the State.

There has been much discussion and debate about the implementation and efficacy of Ecuador's constitutional rights of nature.[28] As Kauffman and Martin observe, "[g]iven the State's plan to fuel economic growth through increased extractivism, including in fragile and protected ecological areas, Ecuador constitutes a 'hard case' for implementing RoN".[29] Certainly, constitutionalising the rights of nature has not prevented the expansion of unsustainable mining in Ecuador. Indeed, in the early years following its 2008 Constitution, the government of Ecuador arrested hundreds of Indigenous and civil society leaders who protested its aggressive plans to increase mining.[30]

Constitutional litigation under Ecuador's rights-of-nature provisions has had mixed success, depending upon the litigants and the political stakes involved. Kauffman and Martin explain that suits in which government actors invoke rights of nature have been uniformly successful.[31] For example, in a particularly draconian mobilisation of the rights of nature, the government succeeded in securing a judicial decision shutting down small-scale illegal mining in the Esmeraldas region; the court ordered the army and police to destroy the tools and equipment used by local miners and the order was promptly carried out.[32]

In a constitutional challenge to the Ministry of Environment's removal of a shrimp farmer from a protected mangrove, the Ministry succeeded in defending its orders, relying in part on rights of nature. In its 2015 decision on appeal, the Constitutional Court held that *buen vivir* and rights of nature are "transversal"[33] and therefore affect all other constitutional rights, including property rights. In language that would be mirrored in rights-of-nature jurisprudence from other jurisdictions, the court noted that Ecuador's constitution takes "a biocentric approach that prioritises Nature in contrast to the classic anthropocentric conception in which the human being is the centre and measure of all things...".[34] Subsequent to this decision, Ecuador enacted a statute granting standing to nature and authorising any person (including the national ombudsman) to represent its interests in court.[35] In answer to Christopher Stone's famous question "Should trees have standing?", environmental law expert Hugo Echevarría eloquently responds: "Today, we can say that, in Ecuador, Nature has full standing and, in fact, mangrove trees had their day in court and won".[36]

Civil society suits directed at local, lower-profile issues have also succeeded under Ecuador's rights-of-nature provisions; however, until recently, suits by civil society litigants have been unsuccessful at preventing high-profile, politicised extractive projects (such as an open pit mine in the Condor-Mirador region of Amazonia).[37] This trend may be changing; in September of 2020, the Cotachi Court issued a constitutional injunction halting copper mining operations in a highly biodiverse cloud forest at Llurimagua that is home to a number of endemic species. The court held that the mining companies' economic rights were superseded by rights of nature, required the Ministry to take corrective action within three months (under the supervision of civil society groups, including universities) and held that if the government could not prove that mining was possible without threatening the extinction of endangered species, the relevant permits would be quashed.[38]

Perhaps most promisingly, Ecuador's Constitutional Court has recently taken the exceptional step of announcing plans to clarify the legal and constitutional content of rights of nature. This is an entirely new panel of the Constitutional Court which took office in 2019 and has signalled a major increase in attention to Ecuador's rights of nature. The court has undertaken to review four cases involving rights of nature (and environmental human rights) in a variety of contexts, including mining in protected areas, oil exploitation and hydroelectric development causing flooding and loss of life. In particular, the court will clarify the relationship between the human right to a healthy environment and the rights of nature.[39]

Like Ecuador, Bolivia's rights-of-nature regime is inspired by the Indigenous concept of *buen vivir*.[40] Bolivia's approach is largely legislative, delineating rights of nature (in even greater detail than in the constitution of Ecuador) in two statutes known as the Rights of Mother Earth Law and the Framework Law for Mother Earth and Integral Development.[41] However, there is some constitutional foundation for rights of nature in Bolivia.[42] The Preamble to Bolivia's constitution provides: "We found Bolivia anew, fulfilling the mandate of our people, with the strength of our Pachamama...",[43] and Article 108 (16) imposes on Bolivians the duty "To protect and defend an environment suitable for the development of living beings".[44]

Moreover, Bolivia's constitutional right to a healthy environment includes a clause that could be seen as extending rights to nonhuman living beings. Article 33 has been translated into English as follows:

> Everyone has the right to a healthy, protected, and balanced environment. The exercise of this right must be granted to individuals and collectives of present and future generations, *as well as to other living things*, so they may develop in a normal and permanent way" [emphasis added].[45]

However, it may also be translated in this way:

> People have a right to a healthy, protected, balanced environment. The exercise of this right allows individuals and communities of present and future generations, as well as other living things, to develop in a normal and permanent manner.[46]

The legal status of Bolivia's constitutional allusions to nonhuman living things is unclear; while the Preamble is clearly nonbinding and the duties section likely aspirational, the "other living things" clause in the right to a healthy environment could potentially have legal force but has yet to be tested in litigation. Bolivian law on the rights of nature remains overwhelmingly statutory.

Outside of Ecuador and Bolivia, rights-of-nature provisions may be found in Australia's Yarra River Protection (*Wilip-gin Birrarung murron*) Act and section 4 of Uganda's Environment Act, 2019;

local rights-of-nature ordinances (of which there are dozens in the United States and Brazil)[47]; and in subnational constitutions. In Mexico, for example, the constitutions of the City of Mexico and the states of Guerrero and Colima contain rights-of-nature provisions.[48] Innovation in this area continues; going beyond rights and legal personality, a remarkably ecocentric city government in Costa Rica city has actually granted citizenship to bees and trees.[49]

New Zealand's celebrated rights-of-nature provisions are embodied in statute but are at least quasi-constitutional in nature since they flow from settlements under the Treaty of Waitangi, which is understood to form part of New Zealand's constitution. New Zealand's foray into rights of nature stemmed from efforts to redress historical and ongoing injustices towards Maori communities and has simultaneously advanced ecological sustainability and Indigenous rights.[50] Following lengthy negotiations with the relevant Maori communities, New Zealand passed the Te Awa Tupua Act in 2017, recognising the personhood of the Whanganui River (*Te Awa Tupua*) with "all the rights, powers, duties, and liabilities of a legal person".[51] The legislation codifies multiple aspects of Maori law and cosmovision, in the Maori language and translated to English.

For example, section 13 codifies the "instrinsic values" of *Te Awa Tupua* including, among others: "*Ko te Awa te mātāpuna o te ora*: the River is the source of spiritual and physical sustenance", and "*Ko au te Awa, ko te Awa ko au*: I am the River and the River is me: the [peoples] of the Whanganui River have an inalienable connection with, and responsibility to, *Te Awa Tupua* and its health and well-being".[52] *Te Awa Tupua* is recognised as "an indivisible and living whole, comprising the Whanganui River from the mountains to the sea, incorporating all its physical and metaphysical elements".[53] Unlike Ecuador's constitutional rights-of-nature provisions, the New Zealand legislation did not set out in any detail the particular rights of the Whanganui River, and indeed Maori negotiators were hesitant to endorse a rights-based approach. Kauffman and Martin explain that "[f]or Whanganui negotiators, the idea of granting their river a [rights-bearing] legal personality was an imperfect approximation of treating the river as a whole, living, spiritual being, but likely the best that could be done within a European legal framework".[54]

Perhaps most importantly,[55] the Te Awa Tupua Act created a guardianship body known as *Te Pou Tupua* comprised of two people, one nominated by the Whanganui Maori people and one by the Crown (which nominated a well-respected Maori leader as its representative).[56] *Te Pou Tupua* is empowered to "to promote and protect the health and well-being of Te Awa Tupua" and must act in the river's best interests.[57] The guardianship body is, in turn, part of a multi-stakeholder watershed management agency. "As a legal person, the river itself is a member of the integrated watershed management body, via its guardians, and thus participates directly in watershed management decisions".[58]

A similar path to rights of nature unfolded with respect to the forest ecosystem and former national park known as Te Urewera, homeland of the Maori Tūhoe iwi (people).[59] Like Te Awa Tupua, recognition of the legal rights and personhood of Te Urewera formed part of a comprehensive settlement between the Crown and a Maori iwi. Moreover, the resulting Act respects and reflects Maori law and cosmovision, characterising Te Urewera in part as follows:

> Section 3
>
> (1) Te Urewera is ancient and enduring, a fortress of nature, alive with history; its scenery is abundant with mystery, adventure, and remote beauty.
>
> (2) Te Urewera is a place of spiritual value, with its own mana [spiritual authority] and mauri [life force].
>
> (3) Te Urewera has an identity in and of itself, inspiring people to commit to its care.
>
> …
>
> (5) For Tūhoe, Te Urewera is their ewe whenua, their place of origin and return, their homeland.
>
> (6) Te Urewera expresses and gives meaning to Tūhoe culture, language, customs, and identity.[60]

Finally, the Act recognises Te Urewera as a "legal entity [with] all the rights, powers, duties, and liabilities of a legal person"[61] and vests responsibility and power in a guardianship body dominated by Maori members (six out of nine beginning in 2017).[62] Although the notion of legal rights was once again unappealing to the Tūhoe negotiators, as Kristi Luke explains,

> Our reason for enabling a legal personality to apply to land was to withdraw the [colonial] law – to filter out the motives, the agendas, the objectives that have been created by somebody else's law…. This legal personality is a piece of law to remove human transactions, human thinking, human self-interest from land in order [to make space for] our Indigenous beliefs,

the care, the kinship, the connectedness.... So Te Urewera is not property.... Te Urewera is not real estate. Te Urewera is my mother. She gives me life and continues to. She is the thing that gives me enjoyment. She reminds me that I am connected to these plants and other creatures, and that I love them, and that they love me.[63]

The guardianship body for Te Urewera has adopted the transformative paradigm of "managing people for the land", a complete turnaround from the New Zealand government's previous approach of managing this ecosystem for the benefit of humans.[64] This has resulted in measurable changes, such as a shift in management of invasive species – replacing harmful pesticides with sustainable local hunting initiatives.[65] Moreover, the official guardianship body has enlisted the help of a respected elder who is now training "bush crews" who will live and work in the forest and report back on its condition and its needs.[66] New Zealand has also committed to recognising the legal personhood of Mount Taranaki and establishing a similar joint guardianship body with the relevant Maori *iwi*.[67]

Summarising their extensive comparative law research, Kauffman and Martin conclude that legal rights-of-nature provisions will be most effective when they "comb[ine] guardianship with collaborative integrated management systems".[68] This approach may not only improve ecological outcomes; it also "promotes a more expansive ecological democracy, [since] as part of the legal implementation of these new rights, governments are devolving legal guardianship to local citizens, often those who have historically been excluded from controlling their own essential ecological resources".[69]

Judge-made rights of nature

Several countries whose constitutions do not include explicit rights-of-nature provisions have nonetheless acquired such constitutional protection through transformative adjudication. The Constitutional Court of Colombia, for example, set a powerful rights-of-nature precedent in a case concerning the egregiously polluted Atrato River basin. Though the region is one of the most biodiverse on Earth,[70] the environmental pressures of unsustainable and illegal extractive activities have severely degraded the Atrato river ecosystem and caused hunger, illness and loss of life among its Indigenous and Afro-Colombian residents (especially children), of whom about 50% live in extreme poverty.[71] The Ombudsman's office had declared a "humanitarian and environmental emergency" in Chocó in 2014, yet the region had been largely "abandoned" by the state, which failed to provide even basic infrastructure for drinking water and sanitation.[72]

In 2016, in response to an *acción de tutela* (a simplified public interest litigation procedure) filed by local communities, the Court held that this situation "threatens the food security of the ethnic communities [and] violates the fundamental rights to a healthy environment, to life, to human dignity, to health, water, territory and culture".[73] In addition, although Columbia's constitution contains no explicit rights-of-nature provision, the Court declared that the Atrato River's "basin and tributaries will be recognized as an entity subject to rights of protection, conservation, maintenance and restoration by the State and ethnic communities"[74] and appointed government and local community representatives to act as legal guardians.[75]

Moreover, the court characterised Colombia's constitution as an "Ecological Constitution" citing about 30 specific provisions including (among others) the right to a healthy environment, the inviolability of the right to life, the state's obligation to protect natural and cultural wealth, and the provision of specific expedited procedures for access to justice in environmental matters.[76] In an eloquent exposition of the ecological purpose of constitutions, the court opined that:

> [t]he biggest challenge of contemporary constitutionalism in environmental matters is to achieve the safeguarding and effective protection of nature, the cultures and life forms associated with it, and biodiversity not by the simple material, genetic or productive utility that these may represent for the human being, but because being a living entity composed of other multiple forms of life and cultural representations, they are subjects of rights.
>
> …
>
> In effect, nature and the environment are a transversal element of the Colombian constitutional order. Its importance lies, of course, in attention to the human beings that inhabit it and the need to have a healthy environment to live a dignified life and in well being conditions, but also in relation to the other living organisms with whom the planet is shared, *understood as stocks worthy of protection in themselves*. It is about being

aware of the interdependence that connects us to all living beings on earth; that is, recognizing ourselves as integral parts of the global ecosystem – biosphere –, rather than from normative categories of domination, simple exploitation or utility [emphasis in original].[77]

Moreover, the court explicitly takes an

eco-centric approach [that] conceives nature as a real subject of rights that must be recognized by the States and exercised under the protection of its legal representatives [namely] by the communities that inhabit nature or that have a special relationship with it.[78]

Indeed, the Colombian court specifically situates nature's rights within a broader framework of "biocultural rights" that recognise the intimate material, cultural and spiritual relationships between the Río Atrato and the Indigenous and Afro-Colombian communities who inhabit the river basin.[79] Thus, the decision evinces a holistic appreciation of the crucial connection between human ecological rights and the rights of nature. Since the *Atrato River* case, four lower-court decisions have similarly declared rights for other rivers and ordered a variety of remedial measures, including orders compelling government to take protective action, prohibitions against pollution and the establishment of guardianship bodies to protect the rivers at issue.[80]

In 2018, the Supreme Court of Colombia went even further, recognising the legal personhood of the Amazon ecosystem. As in the Río Atrato case, the applicants did not argue rights of nature; rather, they alleged that increasing temperatures and ongoing deforestation in the Amazon threatened their rights to a healthy environment, a dignified life, health, food and water.[81] The Court recognised violations of the plaintiffs' rights and those of future generations.[82] Moreover, like the Atrato River judgement, the decision takes a holistic approach to human and ecological rights, holding that:

it is imperative to adopt immediate mitigation measures, and to protect the right to environmental welfare, both of the plaintiffs, and to the other people who inhabit and share the Amazonian territory, not only nationals, but foreigners, together with all inhabitants of the globe, including ecosystems and living beings.[83]

This case once again recognised Colombia's "Ecological Constitution"[84] and found that government had failed to tackle a critical environmental problem, justifying judicial intervention. Thus, "in order to protect this ecosystem vital for our global future, just as the Constitutional Court declared the Atrato river, the Colombian Amazon is recognised as a 'subject of rights', entitled to protection, conservation, maintenance and restoration led by the State and the territorial agencies".[85]

The court ordered local, regional and national bodies to develop, with the participation of the plaintiffs, affected communities and the general population, short-, medium- and long-term action plans to reduce deforestation in the Amazon.[86] Furthermore, the court ordered the Presidency of the Republic and several Ministries (again with public participation) to develop an "intergenerational pact for the life of the Colombian Amazon ... to adopt measures aimed at reducing deforestation to zero".[87] Finally, "within their duties, the defendants [were ordered] to, in the forty-eight hours following the completion of this ruling, increase actions tending to mitigate deforestation while carrying out the modifications contained in the aforementioned mandate".[88]

Like Colombia, India has created constitutional rights of nature through adjudication, building on previous jurisprudence that recognised the human right to a healthy environment despite the absence of any such provision in the text of the Indian constitution. In 2017, the Uttarakhand High Court created new law in two public interest litigation petitions. First, in a case concerning pollution and degradation of the Ganga and Yamuna rivers the court declared these rivers and their tributaries "juristic/legal persons/living entities having the status of a legal person".[89] The court referenced an existing body of case law recognising the juristic personhood of sacred Hindu idols and observed that the Ganga and Yamuna rivers were similarly sacred to Hindus and thus recognition of their legal personhood was necessary "to protect the recognition and the faith of society".[90] Moreover, the court noted the importance of recognising the rivers' legal personhood, given that the government had repeatedly failed to protect and restore them, in default of its constitutional obligation to "endeavor to protect and improve the environment".[91]

In the subsequent *Glaciers* case, the court went further, invoking its *parens patriae* jurisdiction, to declare:

> the Glaciers including Gangotri & Yamunotri, rivers, streams, rivulets, lakes, air, meadows, dales, jungles, forests wetlands,

grasslands, springs and waterfalls, legal entity/legal person/ juristic person/juridical person/moral person/artificial person having the status of a legal person, with all corresponding rights, duties and liabilities of a living person, in order to preserve and conserve them. They are also accorded the rights akin to fundamental rights/ legal rights.... The rights of these legal entities shall be equivalent to the rights of human beings and the injury/harm caused to these bodies shall be treated as harm/injury caused to the human beings.[92]

The court appointed a committee of guardians (*in loco parentis*) for these natural entities, including both independent lawyers and government officials, and issued an order banning mining in the riverbed and directing the removal of illegal encroachments.[93]

Although the Supreme Court later stayed the Uttarakhand High Court's breakthrough rulings on legal personhood,[94] these judgements opened the door to rights of nature in Indian jurisprudence. In a 2018 case concerning the welfare of horses travelling from India to Nepal, the Uttarakhand High Court accorded legal personality and rights to the entire animal kingdom. In a comprehensive and elegant analysis of relevant scientific, philosophical and religious sources, the court concluded that "[n]ew inventions are required to be made in law to protect the environment and ecology"[95] and held:

The entire animal kingdom including avian and aquatic are declared as legal entities having a distinct persona with corresponding rights, duties and liabilities of a living person. All the citizens throughout the State of Uttarakhand are hereby declared persons in loco parentis as the human face for the welfare/protection of animals.[96]

Most recently, in March of 2020, the Punjab and Haryana High Court in India recognised the rights of Sukhna Lake in Chandigarh, declaring it a "legal entity/legal person/juristic person/ juridical person/moral person/artificial person with distinct persona with corresponding rights, duties and liabilities of a living person".[97] The court fined the state governments for knowingly permitting illegal construction and ordered them to declare Sukhna Lake a protected wetland within the meaning of the relevant environmental legislation.[98] It also ordered the demolition of thousands of residential and commercial buildings in the ecologically sensitive catchment area surrounding the lake, but later reversed its demolition order in a second judgement issued in December of 2020.[99]

Like the Bangladeshi decision described below, this case raises the spectre of conflicts between human rights and rights of nature.

The year after India's ambitious rights-of-nature decision on the animal kingdom, Bangladesh broke new legal ground in 2019 when its Supreme Court recognised all of the country's hundreds of rivers as having the status of living persons.[100] Citing rights-of-nature jurisprudence from around the world and noting the severe degradation of Bangladeshi rivers caused by industrial pollution, illegal construction and sand mining, the court appointed the National River Conservation Commission (which was itself created by judicial order in 2009) as guardian of the country's rivers. The court's order includes a robust suite of measures to improve riverine protection and restoration by enhancing the powers of the Commission, punishing illegal developers (by publishing their names and barring them from running for public office or receiving a loan from the national bank) and raising public awareness (through mandatory ecological education at all school levels and in the workplace).[101]

Human rights groups have raised concerns about the millions of people who live in informal settlements along riverbanks and report that authorities have already begun evictions of riverine dwellers in the capital city of Dhaka.[102] The Commission seems open to a holistic approach to river conservation and has stated that "[p]rotecting the rivers also means protecting the entire eco-system, which includes fishermen and farmers who live on the banks. Their rights will also be protected".[103] This case illustrates the crucial importance of taking an integrated approach to rights of nature and environmental human rights, protecting and restoring ecological systems while empowering those who live most intimately with nature.

Limitations on rights of nature

While scholarship and jurisprudence continue to elucidate the necessary components to create an effective constitutional (or legislative) rights-of-nature regime, questions remain about key legal and political issues including: how to ensure that guardians make good faith and effective efforts to protect nature, whether legal personhood and shared guardianship for nature go far enough to respect Indigenous rights of environmental self-determination and how to mobilise adequate resources to end destructive practices and restore the integrity of natural rights-holders. Concerns have also been raised about the potential liability of natural systems and their guardians,[104] but this could be resolved by simply removing "liabilities" from the personhood attributes of natural entities, whether established by courts or enactments, since there is no requirement in law for rights-holders to simultaneously owe obligations (as illustrated by the case of young children and people incapacitated by mental disabilities).

A more difficult question concerns potential conflicts between rights of nature and human rights. While several of the cases illustrated above were win-win in the sense of promoting both human rights (notably the rights of Indigenous peoples) and rights of nature, others raise tensions between the two. Theoretically, any apparent contradiction between human and nature's rights may be resolved by re-conceptualising humans as an integral part of nature, such that human needs and entitlements may be viewed as a component of the rights of nature. Certainly, if we include future generations in the category of human rights-bearers, there is an obvious synergy between human rights and rights of nature – particularly at the ecosystem or biosphere level. Moreover, an abundance of "effective actions are available to simultaneously protect human rights and protect nature".[105]

Nevertheless, any workable approach to rights of nature must recognise that presently existing humans (and all animals) rely on the consumption of other living things for food, shelter and so on, such that recognising rights in natural entities cannot amount to a total prohibition on human encroachment. In this respect, rights of nature may differ from certain human rights – such as the right to life – that are understood to be inviolable. As a result, recognition of rights of nature requires a constant process of line-drawing, determining when and where impingements on the rights of one component of nature (e.g. prey animals) are allowable due to a strong countervailing right or interest on the part of another (e.g. human or nonhuman predators).

One approach to this line-drawing is to recognise an irreducible core of ecosystem or Earth rights that cannot be violated under any circumstances. While the rights of individual plants or animals, or even species, may be justifiably infringed to meet compelling human needs, some theorists insist on a hierarchy of rights wherever large-scale ecological degradation is at issue. For example, Cullinan argues that

> the relationship between humans and Earth … is not a relationship between equals but between the whole and a part. Accordingly, while the needs of the part must be respected, attempting

to balance them against the rights of the whole is inappropri-
ate. The rights of the whole cannot be compromised.[106]

This kind of position is difficult to maintain in the face of human
poverty and suffering such as that experienced by residents of informal riverine settlements in India and Bangladesh or small-scale
illegal miners in Ecuador. Such cases implicate multiple human
rights, including the rights to housing, work, personal security and
development, among others. While the current volume focuses on
domestic constitutional approaches, it should be observed that degrowth and wealth redistribution within and among nations could
allow states to fulfil human needs within ecological limits.[107] Developing nations may require international assistance in order to
implement rights of nature while meeting the legitimate needs of
human populations. For example, Ecuador's proposal to exclude
extractives from large sections of its Amazon region in exchange for
international financial remuneration[108] could have protected rights
of nature in that crucial ecosystem (and environmental human
rights around the world) while allowing the government sufficient
resources to fund poverty alleviation.

In the absence of (or in addition to) international cooperation,
decision-makers will need to find ways of balancing rights of nature
and human rights, just as they currently balance conflicts among
existing human rights when they arise.[109] At a minimum, incursions
into the rights of nature should be subjected to a rigorous justificatory test such as Gerd Winter's notion of "eco-proportionality". In
this conception:

> If an activity encroaches on natural resources: the actor must
> pursue a justifiable societal objective (1); and the activity shall
> prospectively be ... effective, i.e., capable of serving the objec-
> tive (2); necessary, i.e., not replaceable by an alternative that is
> less intrusive on natural resources (3); and balanced, i.e., not
> excessively intrusive on natural resources in view of the impor-
> tance of the societal objective (4).[110]

Another possible approach would be to measure infringements of
rights of nature according to whether the conduct in question complies with Olivia Woolley's "principles of ecological policy-making"
which include, among others: considering all policy alternatives
(rather than limiting analysis to binary "yes-no" assessments
of individual projects in isolation) and reducing consumption/

obviating development where possible (e.g. through energy conservation rather than building new power plants).[111] In particular, decision-makers should "consider whether needs can be satisfied without taking action that will generate [violations of the rights of nature]".[112] Again, this process could be facilitated by international cooperation in capacity-building and technology transfer to assist in the dissemination of sustainable alternatives wherever they exist.

Despite the many challenges and questions that remain,[113] legal recognition of the living personhood of nature may be one of the most powerful ways to "enshrine in [constitutions] the fundamental symbiosis between human and nonhuman ecological health, and to empower suitable stewards who will nurture that symbiosis".[114]

Notes

1 Carla Sbert, *The Lens of Ecological Law: A Look at Mining* (Cheltenham: Edward Elgar, 2020).

2 See, for example, David R Boyd, *The Rights of Nature: A Legal Revolution That Could Save the World* (Toronto: ECW Press, 2017) [Boyd, "Rights of Nature"]; Cameron LaFollette and Chris Maser, *Sustainability and Rights of Nature in Practice* (Boca Raton, FL: CRC Press, 2019) [Lafollette and Maser, "*Sustainability and Rights of Nature* 2020"]; Cameron LaFollette and Chris Maser, eds, *Sustainability and Rights of Nature in Practice* (Abingdon: Routledge, 2020); Alexandre Lilo, "Is Water Simply a Flow? Exploring an Alternative Mindset for Recognizing Water as a Legal Person" (2018) 19:2 VJEL 164 [Lilo, "Is Water Simply a Flow?"]; Nathalie Rühs and Aled Jones, "The Implementation of Earth Jurisprudence through Substantive Constitutional Rights of Nature" (2016) 8:2 Sustainability 174 [Rühs and Jones, "The Implementation of Earth Jurisprudence"].

3 Boyd, "Rights of Nature", *supra* note 2. In addition to promoting sustainability at a broader level, Boyd argues that legal recognition of the rights of nature also help to reduce animal suffering and preserve biodiversity by protecting endangered species. Indeed, a substantial body of animal welfare and endangered species law already exists that implicitly recognises the rights of nature. Though this law is largely codified by statute, the constitutions of at least seven nations, and the European Union's foundational *Treaty of Lisbon*, include provisions identifying the protection of individual animals as a state objective or obligation. Jessica Eisen, "Animals in the Constitutional State" (2017) 15:4 Intl J Const L 909. A further 19 constitutions include provisions relating to the protection of species (variously described as "endangered", "rare", "ecologically sensitive" etc.). See the Constitutions of Ecuador, Egypt, Germany, Hungary, Iceland, Maldives, Slovakia, South Sudan, Switzerland, the UK, Venezuela, Yemen and Zambia.

4 David Takacs, "We Are the River" (2021) 2 University of Illinois L Rev 545; Craig Kauffman, "Managing People for the Benefit of the

Land: Practising Earth Jurisprudence in Te Urewera, New Zealand" (2020) 27:3 ISLE 578 [Kauffman, "Managing People for the Benefit of the Land"].

5 See, for example, Geoffrey Garver, "Are Rights of Nature Radical Enough for Ecological Law?" in Kirsten Anker et al., eds, *From Environmental to Ecological Law* (Abingdon: Routledge, 2021) at 90; Natasha Affolder, "Contagious Environmental Lawmaking" (2019) 31:2 J Envtl L 187 at 207–8.

6 Douglas Deur, Kim Recalma-Clutesi and Clan Chief Kwaxsistalla A Dick, "'When God Put Daylight on Earth, We Had One Voice': Kwakwaka'wakw Perspectives on Sustainability and the Rights of Nature" in Cameron LaFollette and Chris Maser, eds, *Sustainability and Rights of Nature in Practice* (Abingdon: Routledge, 2020) at 89 [Deur et al., "When God Put Daylight on Earth"].

7 See, for example, John Borrows, "Earth-Bound: Indigenous Law and Environmental Reconciliation" in Michael Asch, John Borrows and James Tully, eds, *Resurgence and Reconciliation: Indigenous-Settler Relations and Earth Teachings* (Toronto: University of Toronto Press, 2018) 49 at 82; Leanne B Simpson, *As We Have Always Done: Indigenous Freedom through Radical Resistance* (Minneapolis: University of Minnesota Press, 2017) at 58 [Simpson, "As We Have Always Done"].

8 See, for example, Deur et al., "When God Put Daylight on Earth", *supra* note 6; Jack P Manno and Pamela L Martin, "The Good Life (Sumak Kawsay) and the Good Mind (Ganigonhi:oh): Indigenous Values and Keeping Fossil Fuels in the Ground" in Thomas Princen, Jack P Manno and Pamela L Martin, *Ending the Fossil Fuel Era* (Cambridge, MA: The MIT Press, 2015) 279 at 310.

9 James SY Henderson, "Empowering Treaty Federalism" (1994) 58:2 Sask L Rev 241 at 242. See also Michael Coyle, "Addressing Aboriginal Land Rights in Ontario: An Analysis of Past Policies and Options for the Future – Part I" (2005) 31:2 Queen's LJ 75 at 81; Laura Westra, *Environmental Justice and the Rights of Indigenous Peoples* (Oxford: Routledge, 2013) at 126.

10 Simpson, "As We Have Always Done", *supra* note 7 at 58.

11 John Borrows, "With or Without You: First Nations Law (in Canada)" (1996) 41:3 McGill LJ 629 at 651–2.

12 *Ibid.*

13 See *Ngati Rangi Trust v Manawatu-Wanganui Regional Council* (unreported), [2004] A067/2004 NZEnvC 172 (EC) at paras 109, 318, 320.

14 Fritjof Capra and Ugo Mattei, *The Ecology of Law: Towards a Legal System in Tune with Nature and Community* (Oakland: Berrett-Koehler Publishers, 2015) [Capra and Mattei, "The Ecology of Law"]; Hugo Grotius, *The Rights of War and Peace [De Iure Belli et Pacis Libri Tres]* (1625) (Indianapolis, IN: Liberty Fund, 2005) at II.2.ii.87, 389.

15 See generally Prudence Jones and Nigel Pennick, *A History of Pagan Europe*, 1st ed. (London: Routledge, 1995). See also Capra and Mattei, "The Ecology of Law", *supra* note 14 at 4; Klaus Bosselmann, *The Principle of Sustainability: Transforming Law and Governance* (Abingdon: Routledge, 2017) at 15–16.

16 See, for example, Andreas Wacke, "Protection of the Environment in Roman Law?" (2002) 1 Roman Leg Trad 1.

17 Capra and Mattei, "The Ecology of Law", *supra* note 14.

18 *Ibid* at 52–65.

19 *Ibid* at 56–68.

20 *Ibid* at 74–76.

21 *Ibid* at 87.

22 See Christopher Stone, *Should Trees Have Standing?* (Oxford: Oxford University Press, 2010).

23 See, for example, Rühs and Jones, "The Implementation of Earth Jurisprudence", *supra* note 2; Craig M Kauffman and Linda Sheehan, "Rights of Nature: Guiding Our Responsibilities through Standards" in Stephen Turner et al., eds, *Environmental Rights: The Development of Standards* (Cambridge: Cambridge University Press, 2019) 342 at 366; Gwendolyn J Gordon, "Environmental Personhood" (2018) 43:1 Colum J Envtl L 49; Oliver A Houck, "Noah's Second Voyage: Rights of Nature as Law" (2017) 31:1 Tul Envtl LJ 1; LaFollette and Maser, "*Sustainability and the Rights of Nature 2020*", *supra* note 2; Boyd, "*Rights of Nature*", *supra* note 2.

24 Thomas Berry, "Rights of the Earth: We Need a New Legal Framework Which Recognises the Rights of All Living Beings" in Peter Burdon, ed., *Exploring Wild Law: The Philosophy of Earth Jurisprudence* (Kent Towna: Wakefield Press, 2011) 227 at 229.

25 "The Earth Charter 2000", as reprinted in Klaus Bosselmann and Ronald J Engel, eds, *The Earth Charter: A Framework for Global Governance* (Amsterdam: KIT, 2010) at 257–61.

26 *Harmony with Nature: Report of the UN Secretary General*, UN-GAOR, 72nd Session, UN Doc A/72/175 (2017).

27 Evo M Ayma, *The Rights of Nature: The Case for a Universal Declaration of the Rights of Mother Earth* (Quito: Fundación Pachamama, 2011).

28 See, for example, Louis J Kotzé and Paola V Calzadilla, "Somewhere between Rhetoric and Reality: Environmental Constitutionalism and the Rights of Nature in Ecuador" (2017) 6:3 Transnat'l Envtl L 401; Craig M Kauffman and Pamela L Martin "Can Rights of Nature Make Development More Sustainable? Why Some Ecuadorian Lawsuits Succeed and Others Fail" (2017) 92 World Dev 130 [Kauffman and Martin, "Can Rights of Nature Make Development More Sustainable"]; Erin Daly, "The Ecuadorian Exemplar" (2012) 21:1 RECIEL 63.

29 Kauffman and Martin, "Can Rights of Nature Make Development More Sustainable", *supra* note 28.

30 *Ibid* at 132–3.

31 *Ibid* at 133–9.

32 *Ibid* at 137.

33 Corte Constitucional del Ecuador. (2015). Sentencia No. 166-15-SEP-CC, Caso No. 0507-12-EP at 4.

34 *Ibid* at 10.

35 Hugo Echevarría, "When Courts Meet Nature: A Real Case on Rights of Nature" (18 August 2018), online (blog): *Vermont Journal of Environmental Law* <http://vjel.vermontlaw.edu/courts-meet-nature-real-case-rights-nature/>.

36 *Ibid.*

37 Kauffman and Martin, "Can Rights of Nature Make Development More Sustainable", *supra* note 28 at 136.

38 Global Alliance for the Rights of Nature, "Court Decision on Llurimagua – Rights of Nature Case – Ecuador" (12 November 2020), online: *GARN* <https://therightsofnature.org/court-decision-on-llurimagua-rights-of-nature-case-ecuador/>.

39 Mari Margil, "Constitutional Court Selects Cases to Develop the 'Content' of the Legal Rights of Nature" (17 July 2020), online (blog): *Medium* <https://medium.com/@mari_margil/rights-of-nature-in-ecuador-constitutional-court-selects-cases-to-develop-the-content-of-the-faf2be232547>.

40 Paola V Calzadilla and Louis J Kotzé, "Living in Harmony with Nature? A Critical Appraisal of the Rights of Mother Earth in Bolivia" (2018) 7:3 Transnat'l Envtl L 397 [Calzadilla and Kotzé, "Living in Harmony with Nature?"]. But see Maria Akchurin, "Constructing the Rights of Nature: Constitutional Reform, Mobilization, and Environmental Protection in Ecuador" (2015) 40:4 Law Soc Inq 937 questioning this premise.

41 *Ley de Derechos de la Madre Tierra*, Bolivia 2010, Ley No 071 (Rights of Mother Earth Law). See also the Framework Law, which is more about integral development: *Ley Marco de la Madre Tierra y Desarrollo Integral para Vivir Bien*, Bolivia 2012, Ley No 300 (Framework Law of Mother Earth and Integral Development for Vivir Bien).

42 Joel Colón-Ríos et al., "Constituent Power, the Rights of Nature, and Universal Jurisdiction" (2014) 60:1 McGill LJ 127 at 150 [Colón-Ríos et al., "Constituent Power"].

43 See preamble of *Constitution of the Plurinational State of Bolivia* (7 February 2009) [Bolivian Constitution].

44 *Ibid*, art 108(16); see also Colón-Ríos et al., "Constituent Power", *supra* note 42.

45 Bolivian Constitution, *supra* note 43 at art 33. Calzadilla and Kotzé, "Living in Harmony with Nature?", *supra* note 41 at 401.

46 Colón-Ríos et al., "Constituent Power", *supra* note 42 at 149; The Spanish text is as follows: "Las personas tienen derecho a un medio ambiente saludable, protegido y equilibrado. El ejercicio de este derecho debe permitir a los individuos y colectividades de las presentes y futuras generaciones, además deotros seres vivos, desarrollarse de manera normal y permanente".

47 David R Boyd, "Rights of Nature: Lofty Rhetoric or Revolution?" (2018) 32:4 Nat Res Envtl 13.

48 Since 2006, more than 30 local governments in the United States have drafted local ordinances recognising the rights of nature (Community Environmental Legal Defense Fund 2018). With the help of the NGO Community Environmental Legal Defense Fund, these local groups are mobilising their rights of nature laws to oppose fracking, toxic dumping and other unsustainable practices.

49 Patrick Greenfield, "'Sweet City': The Costa Rica Suburb That Gave Citizenship to Bees, Plants and Trees" (29 April 2020), online: *The Guardian* <www.theguardian.com/environment/2020/apr/29/sweet-city-the-costa-rica-suburb-that-gave-citizenship-to-bees-plants-and-trees-aoe>.

50 See generally Toni Collins and Shea Esterling, "Fluid Personality: Indigenous Rights and the Te Awa Tupua (Whanganui River Claims Settlement) Act 2017 in Aotearoa New Zealand" (2019) 20:1 Melbourne J Intl L 197.

51 Te Awa Tupua (Whanganui River Claims Settlement) Act 2017 (NZ), 2017/7, s 14 [Te Awa Tupua Act 2017].

52 *Ibid*, s 13.

53 *Ibid*, s 12.

54 Craig M Kauffman and Pamela L Martin, "How Courts Are Developing River Rights Jurisprudence: Comparing Guardianship in New Zealand, Colombia, and India" (2019) 20:4 VJEL 260 at 271 [Kauffman and Martin, "How Courts Are Developing River Rights Jurisprudence"]. See also Mesa Cuadros, "The Rivers as Subjects of Rights: Analysis of Comparative Law in the Cases of the Atrato, Whanganui, Vilcabamba, Ganges and Yamuna Rivers" in Gregorio Mesa Cuadros, eds, *Environmental Standard and Environmental Rights in Postpeace Agreements: Some Case Studies* (Bogotá: National University of Colombia, 2019) at 25.

55 See Takacs, "We Are the River", *supra* note 4.

56 Te Awa Tupua Act 2017, *supra* note 51, s 19(1)(c).

57 *Ibid*, s 19(2)(a).

58 Kauffman and Martin, "How Courts Are Developing River Rights Jurisprudence", *supra* note 54 at 272.

59 See generally Kauffman, "Managing People for the Benefit of the Land", *supra* note 4.

60 Te Urewera Act 2014 (NZ), 2014/51.

61 *Ibid*, s 3(3).

62 *Ibid*, s 11(1).

63 Kirsti Luke, "Harmony with Nature" (Presentation Delivered at the United Nations Interactive Dialogue of the General Assembly, United Nations Headquarters in New York, 23 April 2018), quoted in Kauffman, "Managing People for the Benefit of the Land", *supra* note 4 at 586.

64 Kauffman, "Managing people for the benefit of the land", *supra* note 4 at 591–592.

65 *Ibid*.

66 *Ibid* at 590.

67 Eleanor Ainge Roy, "New Zealand gives Mount Taranaki the same legal rights as a person" (22 December 2017), online: *The Guardian* <https://www.theguardian.com/world/2017/dec/22/new-zealand-gives-mount-taranaki-same-legal-rights-as-a-person>.

68 Kauffman and Martin, "How Courts Are Developing River Rights Jurisprudence", *supra* note 4 at 289. See also Cristy Clark et al., "Can You Hear the Rivers Sing? Legal Personhood, Ontology and the Nitty-Gritty of Governance" (2019) 45:4 Ecol LQ 787.

69 Takacs, "We Are the River", *supra* note 4 at 550.

70 *Center for Social Justice Studies et al v Presidency of the Republic et al* [2016], Constitutional Court of Colombia 622/16 at para 1.

71 *Ibid* at paras 2.1–2.4.

72 *Ibid* at para 2.7.

73 *Ibid* at para 9.34.

74 *Ibid* at para 10.2(1).

75 *Ibid.*
76 *Ibid* at paras 5.2–5.5, 9.27–9.32. See also Oscar Darío Amaya Navas, *La Constitución Ecológica de Colombia,* 3rd ed. (Bogotá: Universidad Externado de Colombia).
77 *Ibid* at para 5.10.
78 *Ibid* at para 5.10.
79 See, for example, *Ibid* at para 3.3.
80 Takacs, "We Are the River", *supra* note 4 at 32.
81 *Future Generations v Ministry of the Environment and Others,* [2018] STC4360-3018 (Colombia). See translation by Dejusticia, "Climate Change and Future Generations Lawsuit in Colombia: Key Excerpts from the Supreme Court's Decision" (13 April 2018) at paras 1–2, online: *Dejusticia* <www.dejusticia.org/en/climate-change-and-future-generations-lawsuit-in-colombia-key-excerpts-from-the-supreme-courts-decision/>.
82 *Ibid* at para 11.2.
83 *Ibid* at para 11.3.
84 *Ibid* at para 7.
85 *Ibid* at para 14.
86 *Ibid* at para 14.
87 *Ibid.*
88 *Ibid.*
89 *Mohd Salim v State of Uttarakhand,* [2017] PIL No126 of 2014, 10–11 at para 19 (India) [*Mohd Salim*].
90 *Ibid* at para 16. See also Erin L O'Donnell, "At the Intersection of the Sacred and the Legal: Rights for Nature in Uttarakhand, India" (2018) 30:1 J Envtl L 135.
91 *Mohd Salim, supra* note 39 at para 18.
92 *Lalit Miglani v State of Uttarakhand & others,* [2017] WPPIL 140/2015 (High Court of Uttarakhand).
93 *Ibid.*
94 *State of Uttarakhand & others v Mohd Salim & others,* [2017] Petition for Special Leave to Appeal 016879/2017 (Supreme Court of India) [*State of Uttarakhand*].
95 *Narayan Dutt Bhatt vs Union of India and Others,* [2018] PIL No 43 of 2014 at para 84 (High Court of Uttarakhand).
96 *Ibid* at para 99A.
97 Saurabh Malik, "HC: Sukhna Lake of Chandigarh Is Legal Entity, Raze Buildings in Catchment Area" (3 March 2020), online: *The Tribune India* <https://www.tribuneindia.com/news/chandigarh/hc-sukhna-lake-of-chandigarh-is-legal-entity-raze-buildings-in-catchment-area-50017>.
98 *Ibid.*
99 Rajinder Nagarkoti, "High Court Stays Its Sukhna Catchment Demolition Order" (19 December 2020), online: *Times of India* <https://timesofindia.indiatimes.com/city/chandigarh/high-court-stays-its-sukhna-catchment-demolition-order/articleshow/79805422.cms>.
100 *Human Rights and Peace for Bangladesh vs Bangladesh and Others,* [2019] WP No 13989/2016 (The High Court of Bangladesh).

101 *Ibid.* See also South Asia Network on Dams, Rivers and People, "Bangladesh DRP Overview 2019" (27 January 2020), online: *SANDRP* <https://sandrp.in/2020/01/27/bangladesh-drp-overview-2019/#more-34024>.

102 Rina Chandran, "Fears of Evictions as Bangladesh Gives Rivers Legal Rights" (4 July 2019), online: *Reuters* <https://www.reuters.com/article/us-bangladesh-landrights-rivers/fears-of-evictions-as-bangladesh-gives-rivers-legal-rights-idUSKCN1TZ1ZR>.

103 *Ibid.*

104 *State of Uttarakhand, supra* note 94.

105 See *Report of the Special Rapporteur on the Issue of Human Rights Obligations in Relation to the Enjoyment of a Safe, Clean, Healthy and Sustainable Environment: Human Rights Depend on a Healthy Biosphere*, OHCHR, 75th Session, UN Doc A/75/161 (2020) at 1.

106 Cormac Cullinan, *Wild Law: A Manifesto for Earth Justice*, 2nd ed. (White River Junction, VT: Chelsea Green Publication, 2011) at 100.

107 See generally Carla Sbert, "Needs-based Constraints in an Ecological Law Transition" in Kirsten Anker et al., 1st ed., *From Environmental to Ecological Law* (Abingdon: Routledge, 2021).

108 See Murat Arsel and Natalia A Angel, "'Stating' Nature's Role in Ecuadorian Development: Civil Society and the Yasuni-ITT Initiative" (2012) 28:2 J Dev Soc 203 at 213.

109 See, for example, Hana Mükkerivá, "Right to Environment, Balancing of Competing Interests and Proportionality" (2018) 8:2 Lawyer Q 129.

110 Gerd Winter, "Ecological Proportionality: An Emerging Principle of Law for Nature?" in Christina Voigt, ed., *A Rule of Law for Nature: New Dimensions and Ideas in Environmental Law* (Cambridge: Cambridge University Press: 2013) at 115.

111 Olivia Woolley, *Ecological Governance: Reappraising Law's Role in Protecting Ecosystem Functionality* (Cambridge: Cambridge University Press, 2014) at 71–85.

112 *Ibid* at 73.

113 See also Lilo, "Is Water Simply a Flow?", *supra* note 2 at 189–90.

114 Takacs, "We Are the River", *supra* note 4.

References

Affolder, Natasha, "Contagious Environmental Lawmaking" (2019) 31:2 J Envtl L 187.

Akchurin, Maria "Constructing the Rights of Nature: Constitutional Reform, Mobilization, and Environmental Protection in Ecuador" (2015) 40:4 Law Soc Inq 937.

Amaya Navas, Oscar Darío, *La Constitución Ecológica de Colombia*, 3rd ed. (Bogotá: Universidad Externado de Colombia).

Arsel, Murat & Natalia A Angel, "'Stating' Nature's Role in Ecuadorian Development: Civil Society and the Yasuni-ITT Initiative" (2012) 28:2 J Dev Soc 203.

Ayma, Evo M, *The Rights of Nature: The Case for a Universal Declaration of the Rights of Mother Earth* (Quito: Fundación Pachamama, 2011).

Berry, Thomas, "Rights of the Earth: We Need a New Legal Framework Which Recognises the Rights of All Living Beings" in Peter Burdon, ed., *Exploring Wild Law: The Philosophy of Earth Jurisprudence* (Kent Town: Wakefield Press, 2011) 227.

Bosselmann, Klaus, *The Principle of Sustainability: Transforming Law and Governance* (Abingdon: Routledge, 2017).

Bosselmann, Klaus & Ronald J Engel, eds, *The Earth Charter: A Framework for Global Governance* (Amsterdam: KIT, 2010).

Boyd, David R, *The Rights of Nature: A Legal Revolution That Could Save the World* (Toronto: ECW Press, 2017).

Boyd, David R, "Rights of Nature: Lofty Rhetoric or Revolution?" (2018) 32:4 Nat Res Envtl 13.

Borrows, John, "Earth-Bound: Indigenous Law and Environmental Reconciliation" in Michael Asch, John Borrows & James Tully, eds, *Resurgence and Reconciliation: Indigenous-Settler Relations and Earth Teachings* (Toronto: University of Toronto Press, 2018) 49.

Borrows, John, "With or Without You: First Nations Law (in Canada)" (1996) 41:3 McGill LJ 629.

Calzadilla, Paola V & Louis J Kotzé, "Living in Harmony with Nature? A Critical Appraisal of the Rights of Mother Earth in Bolivia" (2018) 7:3 Transnat'l Envtl L 397.

Capra, Fritjof & Ugo Mattei, *The Ecology of Law: Towards a Legal System in Tune with Nature and Community* (Oakland, CA: Berrett-Koehler Publishers, 2015).

Center for Social Justice Studies et al v Presidency of the Republic et al [2016], Constitutional Court of Colombia 622/16.

Chandran, Rina, "Fears of Evictions as Bangladesh Gives Rivers Legal Rights" (4 July 2019), online: *Reuters* <https://www.reuters.com/article/us-bangladesh-landrights-rivers/fears-of-evictions-as-bangladesh-gives-rivers-legal-rights-idUSKCN1TZ1ZR>.

Clark, Cristy et al., "Can You Hear the Rivers Sing? Legal Personhood, Ontology and the Nitty-Gritty of Governance" (2019) 45:4 Ecol LQ 787.

Collins, Toni & Shea Esterling, "Fluid Personality: Indigenous Rights and the Te Awa Tupua (Whanganui River Claims Settlement) Act 2017 in Aotearoa New Zealand" (2019) 20:1 Melbourne J Intl L 197.

Colón-Ríos, Joel et al., "Constituent Power, the Rights of Nature, and Universal Jurisdiction" (2014) 60:1 McGill LJ 127.

Constitution of the Plurinational State of Bolivia (7 February 2009).

Corte Constitucional del Ecuador. (2015). Sentencia No. 166-15-SEP-CC, Caso No. 0507-12-EP.

Coyle, Michael, "Addressing Aboriginal Land Rights in Ontario: An Analysis of Past Policies and Options for the Future – Part I" (2005) 31:2 Queen's LJ 75.

Cuadros, Mesa, "The Rivers as Subjects of Rights: Analysis of Comparative Law in the Cases of the Atrato, Whanganui, Vilcabamba, Ganges and Yamuna Rivers" in Gregorio M Cuadros, ed., *Environmental Standard and Environmental Rights in Post-peace Agreements: Some Case Studies* (Bogotá: National University of Colombia, 2019).

Cullinan, Cormac, *Wild Law: A Manifesto for Earth Justice*, 2nd ed. (White River Junction, VT: Chelsea Green Publication, 2011).

Daly, Erin, "The Ecuadorian Exemplar" (2012) 21:1 RECIEL 63.

Dejusticia, "Climate Change and Future Generations Lawsuit in Colombia: Key Excerpts from the Supreme Court's Decision" (13 April 2018), online: *Dejusticia* <www.dejusticia.org/en/climate-change-and-future-generations-lawsuit-in-colombia-key-excerpts-from-the-supreme-courts-decision/>.

Deur, Douglas, Kim Recalma-Clutesi & Clan Chief Kwaxsistalla A Dick, "When God Put Daylight on Earth, We Had One Voice': Kwakwaka'wakw Perspectives on Sustainability and the Rights of Nature" in Cameron LaFollette & Chris Maser, eds, *Sustainability and Rights of Nature in Practice* (Abingdon: Routledge, 2020) 89 at 111.

Echevarría, Hugo, "When Courts Meet Nature: A Real Case on Rights of Nature" (18 August 2018), online (blog): *Vermont Journal of Environmental Law* <http://vjel.vermontlaw.edu/courts-meet-nature-real-case-rights-nature/>.

Eisen, Jessica, "Animals in the Constitutional State" (2017) 15:4 Intl J Const L 909.

Future Generations v Ministry of the Environment and Others, [2018] STC4360-3018 (Colombia).

Garver, Geoffrey, "Are Rights of Nature Radical Enough for Ecological Law?" in Kirsten Anker et al., eds, *From Environmental to Ecological Law* (Abingdon: Routledge, 2021) at 90.

Global Alliance for the Rights of Nature, "Court Decision on Llurimagua – Rights of Nature Case – Ecuador" (12 November 2020), online: *GARN* <https://therightsofnature.org/court-decision-on-llurimagua-rights-of-nature-case-ecuador/>.

Gordon, Gwendolyn J, "Environmental Personhood" (2018) 43:1 Colum J Envtl L 49.

Greenfield, Patrick, "'Sweet City': The Costa Rica Suburb That Gave Citizenship to Bees, Plants and Trees" (29 April 2020), online: *The Guardian*<www.theguardian.com/environment/2020/apr/29/sweet-city-the-costa-rica-suburb-that-gave-citizenship-to-bees-plants-and-trees-aoe>.

Grotius, Hugo, *The Rights of War and Peace [De Iure Belli et Pacis Libri Tres]* (1625) (Indianapolis, IN: Liberty Fund, 2005).

Harmony with Nature: Report of the UN Secretary General, UNGAOR, 72nd Session, UN Doc A/72/175 (2017).

Henderson, James SY, "Empowering Treaty Federalism" (1994) 58:2 Sask L Rev 241.

Houck, Oliver A, "Noah's Second Voyage: Rights of Nature as Law" (2017) 31:1 Tul Envtl LJ 1.

Human Rights and Peace for Bangladesh vs Bangladesh and Others, [2019] WP No 13989/2016 (The High Court of Bangladesh).

Jones, Prudence & Nigel Pennick, *A History of Pagan Europe*, 1st ed. (Abingdon: Routledge, 1995).

Kauffman, Craig, "Managing People for the Benefit of the Land: Practising Earth Jurisprudence in Te Urewera, New Zealand" (2020) 27:3 ISLE 578.

Kauffman, Craig M & Pamela L Martin "Can Rights of Nature Make Development More Sustainable? Why Some Ecuadorian Lawsuits Succeed and Others Fail" (2017) 92 World Dev 130.

Kauffman, Craig M & Pamela L Martin, "How Courts Are Developing River Rights Jurisprudence: Comparing Guardianship in New Zealand, Colombia, and India" (2019) 20:4 VJEL 260.

Kauffman, Craig M & Linda Sheehan, "Rights of Nature: Guiding Our Responsibilities through Standards" in Stephen Turner et al., eds, *Environmental Rights: The Development of Standards* (Cambridge: Cambridge University Press, 2019) 342 at 366.

Kotzé, Louis J & Paola V Calzadilla, "Somewhere between Rhetoric and Reality: Environmental Constitutionalism and the Rights of Nature in Ecuador" (2017) 6:3 Transnat'l Envtl L 401.

LaFollette, Cameron & Chris Maser, *Sustainability and Rights of Nature in Practice* (Boca Raton, FL: CRC Press, 2019).

LaFollette, Cameron & Chris Maser, eds, *Sustainability and Rights of Nature in Practice* (Abingdon: Routledge, 2020).

Lalit Miglani v State of Uttarakhand & others, [2017] WPPIL 140/2015 (High Court of Uttarakhand).

Ley de Derechos de la Madre Tierra, Bolivia 2010, Ley No 071 (Rights of Mother Earth Law).

Ley Marco de la Madre Tierra y Desarrollo Integral para Vivir Bien, Bolivia 2012, Ley No 300 (Framework Law of Mother Earth and Integral Development for Vivir Bien).

Lilo, Alexandre, "Is Water Simply a Flow? Exploring an Alternative Mindset for Recognizing Water as a Legal Person" (2018) 19:2 VJEL 164.

Luke, Kirsti, "Harmony with Nature" (Presentation Delivered at the United Nations Interactive Dialogue of the General Assembly, United Nations Headquarters in New York, 23 April 2018).

Malik, Saurabh, "HC: Sukhna Lake of Chandigarh Is Legal Entity, Raze Buildings in Catchment Area" (3 March 2020), online: *The Tribune India* <https://www.tribuneindia.com/news/chandigarh/hc-sukhna-lake-of-chandigarh-is-legal-entity-raze-buildings-in-catchment-area-50017>.

Manno, Jack P & Pamela L Martin, "The Good Life (Sumak Kawsay) and the Good Mind (Ganigonhi:oh): Indigenous Values and Keeping Fossil Fuels in the Ground" in Thomas Princen, Jack P Manno & Pamela L Martin, *Ending the Fossil Fuel Era* (Cambridge, MA: The MIT Press, 2015) 279.

Margil, Mari, "Constitutional Court Selects Cases to Develop the "Content" of the Legal Rights of Nature" (17 July 2020), online (blog): *Medium* <https://medium.com/@mari_margil/rights-of-nature-in-ecuador-constitutional-court-selects-cases-to-develop-the-content-of-the-faf2be232547>.

Mohd Salim v State of Uttarakhand, [2017] PIL No126 of 2014 (India).

Mükkerivá, Hana, "Right to Environment, Balancing of Competing Interests and Proportionality" (2018) 8:2 Lawyer Q 129.

Nagarkoti, Rajinder, "High Court Stays Its Sukhna Catchment Demolition Order" (19 December 2020), online: *Times of India* <https://timesofindia.indiatimes.com/city/chandigarh/high-court-stays-its-sukhna-catchment-demolition-order/articleshow/79805422.cms>.

Narayan Dutt Bhatt vs Union of India and Others, [2018] PIL No 43 of 2014 at para 84 (High Court of Uttarakhand).

Ngati Rangi Trust v Manawatu-Wanganui Regional Council (unreported), [2004] A067/2004 NZEnvC 172 (EC).

O'Donnell, Erin L, "At the Intersection of the Sacred and the Legal: Rights for Nature in Uttarakhand, India" (2018) 30:1 J Envtl L 135.

Report of the Special Rapporteur on the Issue of Human Rights Obligations in Relation to the Enjoyment of a Safe, Clean, Healthy and Sustainable Environment: Human Rights Depend on a Healthy Biosphere, OHCHR, 75th Session, UN Doc A/75/161 (2020).

Roy, Eleanor A, "New Zealand Gives Mount Taranaki the Same Legal Rights as a Person" (22 December 2017), online: *The Guardian* <https://www.theguardian.com/world/2017/dec/22/new-zealand-gives-mount-taranaki-same-legal-rights-as-a-person>.

Rühs, Nathalie & Aled Jones, "The Implementation of Earth Jurisprudence through Substantive Constitutional Rights of Nature" (2016) 8:2 Sustainability 174.

Sbert, Carla, *The Lens of Ecological Law: A Look at Mining* (Cheltenham: Edward Elgar, 2020).

Sbert, Carla, "Needs-based Constraints in an Ecological Law Transition" in Kirsten Anker et al., eds, *From Environmental to Ecological Law*, 1st ed. (Abingdon: Routledge, 2021) 135.

Simpson, Leanne B, *As We Have Always Done: Indigenous Freedom through Radical Resistance* (Minneapolis: University of Minnesota Press, 2017).

South Asia Network on Dams, Rivers and People, "Bangladesh DRP Overview 2019" (27 January 2020), online: *SANDRP* <https://sandrp.in/2020/01/27/bangladesh-drp-overview-2019/#more-34024>.

State of Uttarakhand & others v Mohd Salim & others, [2017] Petition for Special Leave to Appeal 016879/2017 (Supreme Court of India).

Stone, Christopher, *Should Trees Have Standing?* (Oxford: Oxford University Press, 2010).

Takacs, David, "We Are the River" (2021) 2 University of Illinois L Rev 545.

Te Awa Tupua (Whanganui River Claims Settlement) Act 2017 (NZ), 2017/7, s 14.

Te Urewera Act 2014 (NZ), 2014/51.

Wacke, Andreas, "Protection of the Environment in Roman Law?" (2002) 1 Roman Leg Trad 1.

Westra, Laura, *Environmental Justice and the Rights of Indigenous Peoples* (Abingdon: Routledge, 2013).

Winter, Gerd, "Ecological Proportionality: An Emerging Principle of Law for Nature?" in Christina Voigt, ed., *A Rule of Law for Nature: New Dimensions and Ideas in Environmental Law* (Cambridge: Cambridge University Press: 2013) 111.

Woolley, Olivia, *Ecological Governance: Reappraising Law's Role in Protecting Ecosystem Functionality* (Cambridge: Cambridge University Press, 2014).

6 Precaution and non-regression in the ecological constitution

Any ecological constitution must effectively face the problem of scientific uncertainty which pervades all areas of ecological science and environmental law and governance. Despite the efforts of scientists, we do not now – and may never – fully understand how nature works and, in particular, how human processes and products interact with and affect natural systems.[1] While ecological systems have been immensely complex since the beginning of time, the problem is heightened in the current Anthropocene era,[2] in which "humans have added their footprint to nature's complexity",[3] disturbing Earth system functioning to an unprecedented degree. Moreover, as scientists attempt to understand the new Earth that has emerged as a result of human activities, those activities continue to change and evolve.[4] Thus, predicting the probable trajectories of natural systems involves overlaying multiple, complex and ever-changing human and natural phenomena.[5]

The precautionary principle

As the study of ecology has evolved over time, scientists have become increasingly aware of the complexity of natural systems and the difficulty, or even impossibility, of predicting the impacts of anthropogenic disturbances (e.g. habitat destruction, chemical pollution). At the same time, it has become abundantly clear that the case-by-case environmental assessment of specific developments as though each one existed in isolation is a hopelessly inadequate approach to ensuring the well-being of individual ecosystems and Earth systems as a whole.[6] Moreover, a truly precautionary approach recognises that limits to scientific knowledge frequently make it impossible to predict and "manage" natural systems. Instead, "[a] precautionary approach implies a need to focus adaptive management on the management of humans and their social constructs and physical undertakings, rather than on the structure and function of ... ecosystems".[7]

As Woolley explains:

> Broad precautionary measures should be employed that are not reliant on accurate prediction of the effects of activities, but which seek to reduce risks of systemic collapse by reducing the stresses we place on the natural world. For approaches of this nature to be made effective, legal controls are necessary that operate at the macro-level of policy-making.[8]

Constitutional codification is one promising mechanism for infusing an entire legal system with ecological precaution. Although there are numerous different articulations of the precautionary principle in the literature, its basic content is clear: "precautionary decisions are those that prevent damage to health or ecosystems in the face of uncertainty, stimulate the development of more health-protective technologies and activities, and place greater responsibility on proponents of potentially damaging activities".[9] Benidickson adds that "[p]recaution also entails recognition of the importance of leaving wide margins of tolerance or room for manoeuvre to permit natural adaptation to human interference".[10]

Strong versions of the precautionary principle shift the burden of scientific uncertainty to the proponents of industrial activity, requiring producers, emitters and developers to prove the sustainability or safety of their activities in order to justify regulatory approval.[11] One of the strongest and most straightforward instantiations of precaution is the maxim *in dubio pro natura*: "when in doubt, decide in favour of nature".[12] Whatever the language, the obligation is to be cautious in the face of environmental risks rather than waiting for scientific certainty (which often requires the occurrence and documentation of the very harms that are meant to be prevented by environmental law).[13]

In the constitutional context, precaution has a dual role; it both governs how violations of other ecological provisions will be evaluated and provides a substantive independent entitlement or obligation of ecological security.[14] In human rights claims, for example, the precautionary principle suggests that courts should find violations of the right to a healthy environment where environmental harm poses a serious *risk*, rather than requiring claimants to prove causation of actual harm, which may be scientifically impossible.[15] Substantively, the precautionary principle suggests that constitutional guarantees of life, health, personal security, dignity and/or environmental quality include the right not to be experimented on without consent. Thus, for example, states should be prohibited from permitting or facilitating the use and dispersion of poorly understood and potentially toxic chemicals.[16]

Similar conclusions can be drawn with respect to rights of nature; states should take a precautionary approach to assessing threats to nature's rights, *and* nature has the right not to be subjected to uncontrolled experiments (intentionally or unintentionally), testing how much disturbance can be tolerated before the natural system collapses.[17] With respect to sustainability, the precautionary principle requires governments to proactively cultivate ecological integrity,[18] without waiting for conclusive proof of ecological crisis (though such proof is sadly abundant at the global level). Finally, in the context of intergenerational equity, the precautionary principle requires decision-makers to consider reasonable worst-case scenarios in planning for the ecological needs of future generations. Thus, precaution complements nearly every imaginable element in an ecological constitution and should be adopted – in its most robust forms – by ecologically literate legislators, officials and adjudicators.

Finally, an inclusive, rights-respecting approach to the precautionary principle (and all principles of ecological law and governance) would incorporate Indigenous Traditional Knowledge.[19] Ecological trends that may not yet be visible in Western scientific data may already be appreciated by Indigenous knowledge-keepers.[20] This approach is being lived by Maori stewards of the Te Urewera (a mountain ecosystem recognised as a legal person in 2014), who have deployed "bush crews" who live in and "listen to" the forest, reporting back to the official guardianship body regarding its condition and needs.[21]

Precautionary provisions in national constitutions

As Sachs has noted, despite debates regarding the precise definition and scope of the precautionary principle, precaution does provide important guidance for regulatory action in various contexts.[22] As a result, it makes sense to include such a principle in constitutions, and a small but significant number of nations have done so.

For example, Zambia's constitution adopts a common definition of the precautionary principle, declaring that one of the principles governing environmental management in that country is the following: "...where there are threats of serious or irreversible damage to the environment, lack of full scientific certainty shall not be used as a reason for postponing cost-effective measures to prevent environmental degradation".[23] The 2016 constitution of Côte d'Ivoire codifies a stronger version of precaution, providing: "Where there may be a risk of harm that could seriously and irreversibly affect the environment, the State and public communities are required to assess the potential harm and to adopt the necessary preventive measures by applying the precautionary principle". Similarly, the French *Charte de l'environnement*[24] provides that as soon as a threat of serious or irreversible environmental harm emerges, and despite scientific uncertainty, "public authorities should monitor, by the application of the precautionary principle in their relevant domains, the implementation of risk assessment procedures and the adoption of proportionate, provisional measures in order to prevent the realisation of the damage".[25]

Ecuador includes precaution in multiple provisions of its 2008 constitution. Article 397 on the right to a healthy environment provides as follows:

> To guarantee the individual and collective right to live in a healthy and ecologically balanced environment, the State pledges: To permit any [person] to file legal proceedings and resort to judicial and administrative bodies without detriment to their direct interest, to obtain from them effective custody in environmental matters, including the possibility of requesting precautionary measures that would make it possible to end the threat or the environmental damage that is the object of the litigation. The burden of proof regarding the absence of potential or real danger shall lie with the operator of the activity or the defendant.[26]

Article 73 further provides that: "The State shall apply preventive and restrictive measures on activities that might lead to the extinction of species, the destruction of ecosystems and the permanent alteration of natural cycles".[27] Finally, Article 395 specifically codifies the maxim *in dubio pro natura*: "In the event of doubt about the scope of legal provisions for environmental issues, it is the most favorable interpretation of their effective force for the protection of nature that shall prevail".[28]

Case law

Ecuadorian jurisprudence has confirmed and enforced the principle of *in dubio pro natura* codified in its constitution. In a case involving damage to a river, for example, the Court held that:

> until it can be shown that there is no probability or danger to the environment of the kind of work that is being done in a specific place, it is the duty of constitutional judges to immediately guard and to give effect to the constitutional right of nature, doing what is necessary to avoid contamination or to remedy it.[29]

Similarly, "[i]n Brazil, Costa Rica, Indonesia, and Pakistan, courts have employed the principle [of *in dubio pro natura*] to construe statutes in favor of interpretations that promote ecological integrity".[30]

In a famous Colombian case concerning "biocultural" human rights and the rights of nature, the precautionary principle was applied in assessing violations of several eco-constitutional provisions.[31] This followed previous Colombian precedents, for example a case in which the court ordered the Ministry of Information and Communications Technologies to dismantle a telecommunications antenna near the applicant's home and to "to regulate … in accordance with the precautionary principle, the prudent distance between mobile telephone towers and homes, educational institutions, hospitals and geriatric homes".[32]

Canadian courts have also adopted the precautionary principle. In *Haida Nation v. Canada*, the Federal Court of Canada granted an injunction to an Indigenous nation suspending the 2015 commercial herring fishery in Haida Gwaii, British Colombia (the lands and waters of which are subject to a constitutional Indigenous title suit that has been characterised by the Supreme Court of Canada as a strong prima facie claim).[33] The court recognised the unique ecological values of the area, the strength of the Haida's claim to title and the depth of scientific uncertainty surrounding sustainable harvest levels in the fishery at issue. Taking a precautionary approach, it held that irreparable harm would ensue if the Department of Fisheries and Oceans permitted commercial fishing in the area at issue. In another case, the Supreme Court of Canada referred to the precautionary principle in upholding a municipal ban on nonessential pesticides, despite the absence of conclusive proof of toxicity.[34]

Thus, case law involving *in dubio pro natura* and the precautionary principle demonstrates that constitutional protection for precaution can result in improved judicial and ecological outcomes.

The non-regression principle

A close correlate of the precautionary principle is the principle of non-regression, defined as a prohibition on state acts or omissions that result in ecological degradation (e.g. degradation in air quality, water quality, biodiversity) or in laws aimed at ecological preservation or restoration.[35] Non-regression has both a substantive and juridical component; in its most robust form, the principle protects both ecological quality and regulatory environmental standards.

The principle of non-regression may be a key solution to the problem of uncertainty in environmental regulation. Rather than requiring plaintiffs to prove harm or risk, as other approaches do, a claim based on infringement of the non-regression principle would simply require evidence that the impugned state action represents a reduction in environmental protection compared to its predecessor. In some cases, it could be as simple as comparing the numbers in emissions limits and noting that the impugned one is higher than its previous version.

Non-regression finds strong support in both international human rights law and international environmental law and has been applied in a number of domestic constitutional contexts.[36] For example, in Ecuador's constitution, the state pledges "To strengthen the harmonization of national legislation with [environmental] rights and regimes ... in accordance with the principles of progressivity and non-regression".[37] The Constitution of Bhutan includes a very strong substantive non-regression provision, guaranteeing that "a minimum of sixty percent of Bhutan's total land shall be maintained under forest cover for all time".[38]

Constitutional case law has also recognised the principle of non-regression. In Belgium, for example, the constitutional right to a healthy environment has been interpreted as including a "standstill" obligation presumptively prohibiting the legislature from revising environmental laws in a way that reduces the level of protection currently provided.[39] In one case, the court ruled that an attempt to relax noise regulations to enable motor vehicle racing violated the standstill aspect of the right to a healthy environment.[40] Similarly, in Hungary, in cases challenging the privatisation of forests and proposed development in a nature reserve, the

Constitutional Court held that "the implementation of the right to environment requires not only keeping the present level of protection, but also that the state should not step backward".[41]

In Brazil, the non-regression principle has been used to challenge the constitutionality of a reduction in the territory of a state park (among other things). The federal Public Prosecutor has opined that [translation] "the principle of the prohibition of ecological regression signifies that, unless there are changes in material facts, reductions in the level of protection previously provided are prohibited".[42] In 2012, Costa Rica's Constitutional Court articulated the principle of non-regression as a substantive guarantee of environmental rights that prohibits the state from adopting laws, policies or standards that reduce environmental protection without compelling justification.[43] In Argentina, a court struck down legislative amendments weakening regulation of aerial pesticide spraying on the basis that it violated the principle of non-regression.[44] Courts in the US states of Montana and Pennsylvania have also struck down legislative provisions weakening ecological protections as violations of those states' (subnational) constitutional environmental rights.[45]

To summarise, the principles of precaution, *in dubio pro natura* and non-regression constitute promising mechanisms for ensuring the efficacy of other eco-constitutional provisions that could potentially be undermined by the problem of scientific uncertainty. Although courts may voluntarily adopt such principles as interpretive aids, there is a strong argument for explicit textual codification in order to guide both judicial and government decision-making at all levels.

Notes

1 See Brian A. Maurer, "Ecological Complexity" in Robert A Meyers, ed., *Encyclopedia of Complexity and Systems Science* (New York: Springer, 2009).

2 See Louis J Kotzé, "Rethinking Global Environmental Governance in the Anthropocene (2014) 32 J Energy Nat Res L 121; Louis J Kotzé and Rakhyun E Kim, "Earth System Law: The Juridical Dimensions of Earth System Governance" (2019) 1 Earth Syst Gov 1 at 2–3.

3 Walter R Erdelen and Jacques G Richardson, *Managing Complexity: Earth Systems and Strategies for the Future: Earth Systems and Strategies for the Future* (Boca Raton, FL: Routledge, 2018) at 16.

4 See e.g. Sarah Burch et al., "New Directions in Earth System Governance Research" (2019) 1 Earth Syst Gov 100006.

5 See Louis J Kotzé, "Earth System Law for the Anthropocene: Rethinking Environmental Law alongside the Earth System Metaphor" (2020) 11 Transnat'l Legal Theory 75.

6 See e.g. Rakhyun E Kim and Brendon Mackey, "International Environmental Law as a Complex Adaptive System" (2014) 14 Int Envtl Agreements 5.

7 Geoffrey Garver, *Ecological Law and the Planetary Crisis: A Legal Guide for Harmony on Earth* (Abingdon: Routledge, 2020) at 112.

8 Olivia Woolley, *Ecological Governance: Reappraising Law's Role in Protecting Ecosystem Functionality* (Cambridge: Cambridge University Press, 2014) at 38 [Woolley, *Ecological Governance*]. See also Nicholas A Robinson, "The Resilience Principle (2014) 5 IUCN Acad Envtl L eJournal 19.

9 Marco Martuzzi and Joel A Tickner, *The Precautionary Principle: Protecting Public Health, the Environment and the Future of Our Children* (Copenhagen: World Health Organization: Europe, 2004).

10 Jamie Benidickson, *Environmental Law*, 2nd ed. (Toronto: Irwin Law Inc., 2002) at 22, citing T O'Riordan and J Cameron, *Interpreting the Precautionary Principle* (London: Earthscan Publications, 1994) at 16–18.

11 See Noah M Sachs, "Rescuing the Strong Precautionary Principle from Its Critics" (2011) U Ill L Rev 1285 [Sachs, "Rescuing the Strong Precautionary Principle from Its Critics"].

12 Nicholas s Bryner, "An Ecological Theory of Statutory Interpretation" (2018) 54 Idaho L Rev 3 at 25; see also Josefina Russo and Ricardo Russo, "*In Dubio Pro Natura:* Un Principio de Precaución y Prevención a Favor de los Recursos Naturales (2009) 5 Tierra Trop 1659.

13 See Paul Harremoës et al., eds, *The Precautionary Principle in the 20th Century: Late Lessons from Early Warnings* (London: Earthscan Publications, 2002).

14 See generally, Lynda M Collins, "Security of the Person, Peace of Mind: A Precautionary Approach to Environmental Uncertainty" (2013) 4:1 J Hum Rts Envtl 79.

15 *Ibid.*

16 *Ibid.*

17 Woolley, *Ecological Governance, supra* note 8 at 8–10, 38.

18 See generally, Laura Westra et al., *Ecological Integrity in Science and Law* (Cham: Springer, 2020).

19 Fran Trippett, *A Functional Role for Indigenous Knowledge Systems (TEK) within Decision-Making Structures* (LLM Thesis) (Halifax: Dalhousie University, 2000); Ashli Akins et al., "The Universal Precautionary Principle: New Pillars and Pathways for Environmental, Sociocultural and Economic Resilience" (2019) 11:8 Sustainability 2357.

20 See e.g. E Weatherhead et al., "Changes in Weather Persistence: Insights from Inuit Knowledge" (2010) 20 Global Envtl Change 523 at 523.

21 Craig Kauffman, "Managing People for the Benefit of the Land: Practising Earth Jurisprudence in Te Urewera, New Zealand" (2020) 27:3 ISLE 578 at 590.

22 Sachs, "Rescuing the Strong Precautionary Principle from Its Critics", *supra* note 11 at 1310 *et seq.*

23 *Constitution of Zambia* (1991), Article 255.

24 *Charte de l'environnement de France* (2004).
25 *Ibid* at art 5.
26 *Constitution of 2008 of the Republic of Ecuador* (20 October 2008) at art 73.
27 *Ibid* at art 73.
28 *Ibid* at art 395.
29 *Wheeler c. Director de la Procuraduria General Del Estado de Loja* 2011.
30 Nicholas s Bryner, "An Ecological Theory of Statutory Interpretation" (2018) 54 Idaho L Rev 3 at 29.
31 See *Center for Social Justice Studies et al. v. Presidency of the Republic et al.* Judgment T-622/16, Constitutional Court of Colombia (10 November 2016).
32 See *Center for Social Justice Studies et al. v. Presidency of the Republic et al.* Judgment T-622/16, Constitutional Court of Colombia (10 November 2016) at para 7.37–7.38.
33 *Haida Nation v. Canada (Minister of Fisheries and Oceans)*, [2015] F.C.J. No 281, 2015 FC 290 (F.C.).
34 *114957 Canada Ltée (Spraytech, Société d'arrosage) v. Hudson (Town)*, [2001] 2 S.C.R. 241.
35 See generally, Michel Prieur and Gonzalo Sozzo, eds, *La non régression en droit de l'environnement* (Brussels: Bruylant, 2013); Michel Prieur, "Non-regression in Environmental Law" (2012) 5:2 IUCN Commissions SAPIENS.
36 See generally Lynda Collins, "Non-regression" in Jean-Frédéric Morin and Amandine Orsini, eds, *Essential Concepts of Global Environmental Governance* (Abingdon: Routledge, 2020); Isabel Hachez, *Le principe de standstill dans le droit des droits fondamenteaux: une irreversibilité relative* (Brussels: Bruylant, 2008) [Hachez, *Le principe de standstill dans le droit des droits fondamenteaux*].
37 *Constitution of Ecuador* at art 423 para 3.
38 *Constitution of Bhutan* at art 5 para 3.
39 See Hachez, Hachez, *Le principe de standstill dans le droit des droits fondamenteaux, supra* note 36.
40 *Jacobs v. Flemish Region* (1999) Council of State No 80.018, 29 April 1999, cited in Boyd, *The Environmental Rights Revolution* at 224.
41 Constitutional Court, Judgment 28/1994 and Judgment 48/1997 (Hungary), cited in Boyd, *The Environmental Rights Revolution* at 196.
42 See Action of Unconstitutionality No 14.661/2009 (Brazil).
43 Constitutional Chamber of the Supreme Court of Justice, Resolution 2012-13367 (Costa Rica).
44 *Picorelli et al. v Municipality of General Pueyrredon*, Ordinance No 21.296 of 2013 (Argentina).
45 Lynda M Collins and David Boyd, "Non-Regression and the *Charter* Right to a Healthy Environment" (2016) 29 J Envtl L Prac 285 at 299–300.

References

114957 Canada Ltée (Spraytech, Société d'arrosage) v Hudson (Town), 2001 SCC 40.

Action of Unconstitutionality, 26 March 2009, No 14.661/2009 (Brazil).

Akins, Ashli et al., "The Universal Precautionary Principle: New Pillars and Pathways for Environmental, Sociocultural and Economic Resilience" (2019) 11:8 Sustainability 2357.

Benidickson, Jamie, *Environmental Law*, 2nd ed. (Toronto: Irwin Law Inc., 2002).

Boyd, David R, *The Environmental Rights Revolution: A Global Study of Constitutions, Human Rights, and the Environment* (Vancouver: UBC Press, 2012).

Bryner, Nicholas S, "An Ecological Theory of Statutory Interpretation" (2018) 54:1 Idaho L Rev 3.

Burch, Sarah et al., "New Directions in Earth System Governance Research" (2019) 1 Earth Syst Gov 100006.

Collins, Lynda, "Principle of Non-regression" in Jean-Frédéric Morin & Amandine Orsini, eds, *Essential Concepts of Global Environmental Governance*, 2nd ed. (Oxon: Routledge, 2020) 205.

Collins, Lynda M, "Security of the Person, Peace of Mind: A Precautionary Approach to Environmental Uncertainty" (2013) 4:1 J Hum Rts Envtl 79.

Collins, Lynda M & David R Boyd, "Non-Regression and the *Charter* Right to a Healthy Environment" (2016) 29 J Env L Prac 285.

Constitution of 2008 of the Republic of Ecuador (20 October 2008).

Constitution of the Kingdom of Bhutan (18 July 2008).

Constitution of Zambia (24 August 1991).

Constitutional Chamber of the Supreme Court of Justice, Resolution 2012–13367 (Costa Rica).

Constitutional Court of Columbia, 10 November 2016, *Center for Social Justice Studies v Presidency of the Republic*, Judgment T-622/16 (Columbia).

Constitutional Court, Judgment 28/1994, V.20 AB (Hungary).

Constitutional Court, Judgment 48/1997, (X. 6.) AB Decision (Hungary).

Corte Provincial de Justicia de Loja [Provincial Court of Justice of Loja], 30 March 2011, *Wheeler c Director de la Procuraduria General Del Estado en Loja*, Juicio No 11121-2011-0010, Casillero No 826 (Ecuador).

Council of State, Brussels, 29 April 1999, *Jacobs v Flemish Region* (1999), Council of State No 80.018, cited in David R Boyd, *The Environmental Rights Revolution: A Global Study of Constitutions, Human Rights, and the Environment* (Vancouver: UBC Press, 2012).

Erdelen, Walter R & Jacques G Richardson, *Managing Complexity: Earth Systems and Strategies for the Future* (New York: Routledge, 2019).

Garver, Geoffrey, *Ecological Law and the Planetary Crisis: A Legal Guide for Harmony on Earth* (London: Routledge, 2020).

Hachez, Isabel, *Le principe de standstill dans le droit des droits fondamenteaux: une irreversibilité relative* (Brussels: Bruylant, 2008).

Haida Nation v Canada (Fisheries and Oceans), 2015 FC 290.

Harremoës, Paul et al., eds, *The Precautionary Principle in the 20th Century: Late Lessons from Early Warnings* (Oxon: Earthscan, 2002).

Kauffman, Craig M, "Managing People for the Benefit of the Land: Practising Earth Jurisprudence in Te Urewera, New Zealand" (2020) 27:3 ISLE 578.

Kim, Rakhyun E & Brendan Mackey, "International Environmental Law as a Complex Adaptive System" (2014) 14:1 Intl Envtl Agreements 5.

Kotzé, Louis J, "Earth System Law for the Anthropocene: Rethinking Environmental Law alongside the Earth System Metaphor" (2020) 11:1/2 Transnat'l Leg Theory 75.

Kotzé, Louis J, "Rethinking Global Environmental Law and Governance in the Anthropocene" (2014) 32:2 J Energy Nat Res L 121.

Kotzé, Louis J & Rakhyun E Kim, "Earth System Law: The Juridical Dimensions of Earth System Governance" (2019) 1 Earth Syst Gov 100003.

La Plata, 24 September 204, *Picorelli v Municipality of General Pueyrredon*, Ordinance No 21.296/2013 (Argentina).

Loi constitutionnelle n°2005–205 du 1er mars 2005 relative à la Charte de l'environnement, JO 2004.

Martuzzi, Marco & Joel Tickner, *The Precautionary Principle: Protecting Public Health, the Environment and the Future of Our Children* (Copenhagen: WHO Regional Office for Europe, 2004).

Maurer, Brian A, "Ecological Complexity" in Robert A Meyers, ed., *Encyclopedia of Complexity and Systems Science* (New York: Springer, 2009) 2697.

O'Riordan, Timothy & James Cameron, *Interpreting the Precautionary Principle* (Oxon: Earthscan, 1994).

Prieur, Michel, "Non-regression in Environmental Law" (2012) 5:2 SAPIENS 52.

Prieur, Michel & Gonzalo Sozzo, eds, *La non régression en droit de l'environnement* (Brussels: Bruylant, 2012).

Robinson, Nicholas A, "The Resilience Principle" (2014) 5 IUCN Acad Envtl L J 19.

Russo, Josefina & Ricardo Russo, "In Dubio Pro Natura: Un Principio de Precaución y Prevención a Favor de los Recursos Naturales" (2009) 5:1 Tierra Trop 23.

Sachs, Noah M, "Rescuing the Strong Precautionary Principle from Its Critics" (2011) 4 U Ill L Rev 1285.

Trippett, Fran, *Towards a Broad-Based Precautionary Principle in Law and Policy: A Functional Role for Indigenous Knowledge Systems (TEK) within Decision-Making Structures* (LLM Thesis, Dalhousie University, 2000).

Weatherhead, E, S Gearheard & RG Barry, "Changes in Weather Persistence: Insights from Inuit Knowledge" (2010) 20 Global Envtl Change 523.

Westra, Laura, Klaus Bosselmann & Matteo Fermeglia, eds, *Ecological Integrity in Science and Law* (Cham: Springer, 2020).

Woolley, Olivia, *Ecological Governance: Reappraising Law's Role in Protecting Ecosystem Functionality* (Cambridge: Cambridge University Press, 2014).

7 Ecological constitutionalism in a changing climate

Thus far, this volume has focused upon overarching legal rights, duties and principles that make up the building blocks of an ecological constitution. However, the framers of such constitutions should also consider including guarantees pertaining to specific ecological processes and spaces that are crucial to the success and survival of their societies. Many constitutions already protect access to clean water,[1] and all states should consider specifically protecting the right to clean air.[2] Moreover, in order to meaningfully advance ecological sustainability, constitutions should attempt to preserve Earth system functioning to the extent possible in a domestic context. In this respect, the concept of planetary boundaries may be of great assistance.

Developed by a group of leading scientists in the first decade of the 21st century, the planetary boundaries framework describes specific, serious threats to Earth system functioning and identifies parameters for evaluating such threats using numerical limits wherever possible.[3] By applying a precautionary approach to the best available science, planetary boundaries seek to delineate a "'safe operating space' for global societal development".[4] If we transgress one or more of the boundaries, we risk transitioning "to a very different state of the Earth system, one that is likely to be much less hospitable to the development of human societies".[5]

Planetary boundaries have been identified for nine critical threats to Earth System processes: stratospheric ozone depletion; chemical pollution and introduction of novel entities; ocean acidification; freshwater overconsumption and human pressure on the global hydrological cycle; land system change; disruptions to biogeochemical flows (particularly Nitrogen and Phosphorous flows); atmospheric aerosol loading; loss of biosphere integrity (including declining biodiversity and increasing extinctions); and climate change.[6] The latter two have now been identified as "core" boundaries; a sustained transgression of either of these could, by itself, cause profound changes in the state of the Earth system with sobering consequences for human beings (and countless other Earth-dwellers).[7]

Legal thinkers have proposed translating planetary boundaries into legal rules and institutions in a variety of ways both nationally and internationally.[8] While the status and content of a truly *global* ecological constitution[9] delineated by planetary boundaries are beyond the scope of this book, it seems clear that the guarantee of a "safe operating space" for humanity should be viewed as a consensus goal of legal systems at all levels. Although it may be difficult to "scale down" planetary boundaries to the national level,[10] the concept suggests, at a minimum, that ecological constitutions should pay particular attention to crucial earth systems that underlie sustainability both locally and globally.

Given its core nature, and the degree of urgency involved (since this boundary has already been crossed),[11] climate change is an ecologically obvious place to start.[12] Moreover, the human rights orientation of constitutions worldwide also justifies specific inclusion of climate provisions, since "[c]limate change is having a major impact on a wide range of human rights today, and could have a cataclysmic impact in the future unless ambitious actions are undertaken immediately".[13]

Climate provisions in national constitutions

Since the late 1990s, a small but growing number of countries around the world have responded to the climate emergency by amending their constitutions to include climate-related provisions, though most of these appear to be nonbinding. For example, 1998 amendments to the Dominican Republic's constitution recognise as "a priority of the State" the legal formulation and execution of a "plan of territorial ordering that ensures the efficient and sustainable use of the natural resources of the Nation, in accordance with the necessity of adaptation to climate change".[14] Viet Nam's constitution sets out a "state policy" to "tak[e] initiative in prevention and resistance against natural calamities and response to climate change".[15]

The constitutions of Côte D'Ivoire[16] and the 2020 draft Constitution of Algeria both include mention of climate change in their Preambles. Thailand's 2017 constitution states that national reform must seek to achieve the "objective" of (*inter alia*) "having a water resource management system which is efficient, fair and sustainable, with due regard given to every dimension of water demand in combination with environmental and climate change".[17] Recognising the global nature of climate change, Cuba's constitution states that in its international relations, the state

> Promotes the protection and conservation of the environment as well as responding to climate change, which threatens the survival of the human species, through the recognition of common, yet differential, responsibilities ... as well as the eradication of irrational patterns of production and consumption.[18]

Stronger constitutional approaches to climate change are framed in terms of state obligations and/or individual rights. For example, a 1999 amendment to the Venezuelan constitution establishes a "fundamental duty of the state ... to ensure that the populace develops in a pollution-free environment in which air, water, soil, coasts, climate, the ozone layer and living species receive special protection, in accordance with law".[19] Zambia's constitution provides that the state "shall ... establish and implement mechanisms that address climate change".[20] Tunisia is currently unique in constitutionalising a procedural right related to climate change. Article 45 of its 2016 constitution "guarantees the right to a healthy and balanced environment and the right to participate in the protection of the climate".[21]

Not surprisingly, Ecuador's constitution includes multiple climate-relevant provisions, anchored by Article 414 which provides that:

> [t]he State shall adopt adequate and cross-cutting measures for the mitigation of climate change, by limiting greenhouse gas emissions, deforestation, and air pollution; it shall take measures for the conservation of the forests and vegetation; and it shall protect the population at risk.[22]

This article is complemented by others promoting *inter alia* renewable energy,[23] forest conservation[24] and a "sustainable environment".[25] Similar to these more specific provisions, Bhutan's constitutional commitment to preserve 60% of its forest cover in perpetuity is arguably another example of climate constitutionalism (given the importance of forests in climate regulation).[26]

The explicit climate-related provisions described above are largely untested. While Tunisia's procedural right is a good first step, the obvious gap in climate constitutionalism around the world is the absence of clear, substantive constitutional rights related to a safe climate. One straightforward way to remedy this situation in states with a constitutional right to a healthy environment would be to add a section adopting the UN Special Rapporteur's definition of the "substantive elements" of environmental rights, including "healthy ecosystems and biodiversity[;] a safe climate, clean air, clean water and non-toxic environments".[27] Alternatively, states could add a separate right to a safe, healthy and sustainable climate, buttressed by access to justice provisions empowering citizens to require effective regulatory responses.

Case law

In the absence of clearly justiciable constitutional climate rights or obligations, a number of courts around the world have recognised climate guarantees within other rights. In its 2015 decision in *Leghari v the Federation of Pakistan*,[28] for example, the Lahore High Court held that the state's failure to implement its national climate change framework policy violated citizens' fundamental constitutional rights to life and dignity. In an eloquent passage, Justice Syed Mansoor Ali Shah (now a judge of the Supreme Court of Pakistan) held:

> Climate Change is a defining challenge of our time and has led to dramatic alterations in our planet's climate system. For Pakistan, these climatic variations have primarily resulted in heavy floods and droughts, raising serious concerns regarding water and food security. On a legal and constitutional plane this is a clarion call for the protection of fundamental rights of the citizens of Pakistan, in particular, the vulnerable and weak segments of the society who are unable to approach this Court.[29]

Justice Shah invoked the court's mandamus jurisdiction to summon the Joint Secretary for Climate Change as well as a Climate Change Focal person from each ministry, department and authority of the government. He then constituted a Climate Change Commission and supervised its activities in a series of 25 further hearings before dissolving it in a final hearing in 2018.[30] Justice Shah concluded that the work of the Commission had been successful in "sensitizing" the government and had achieved roughly 66% of its assigned goals. However, the Court retained jurisdiction over the matter and may be called upon in future if government regresses in its climate policy in a way that threatens fundamental rights.[31]

While this level of judicial intervention may be viewed as excessive in some legal traditions, it reflects established practice in South Asia (and Latin America),[32] particularly in cases involving government inaction in the face of extreme environmental harm.[33] Barritt and Sediti note that the impacts of climate change in the Pakistan (and elsewhere in the Global South) are already "live and devastating"; thus, "[d]eveloping an appropriate judicial response in situations of urgency will ... look quite different to the response in jurisdictions where the devastation of climate change still seems distant".[34]

In *Earthlife Africa Johannesburg v Minister of Environmental Affairs* (2017), the South African judiciary entered the world of climate law, holding that – despite the absence of any explicit statutory requirement – the environmental assessment of a large coal-fired power plant had to consider climate implications. Although the outcome was largely based on statute, it was almost certainly influenced by section 24 of South Africa's constitution which includes both a substantive environmental right and an ecological trusteeship obligation on government.[35]

In its revolutionary decision in the 2018 *Amazonia* case, the Supreme Court of Colombia found that government conduct and inaction in relation to deforestation in the Amazon violated multiple provisions in Colombia's "ecological constitution".[36] It noted as imperatives "the preservation of this ecosystem for its importance in regulating the global climate ... and to confront climate change, given the destruction of the amazon forest in the national territory".[37] In addition to its ground-breaking order recognising the legal personhood of the Colombian Amazon, the court found that climate change violates intergenerational equity[38] and ordered local, regional and national bodies to develop, with the participation of the plaintiffs, affected communities and the general population, short-, medium- and long-term action plans to reduce deforestation in the Amazon.[39] Furthermore, it ordered the Presidency of the Republic and several Ministries (again with public participation) to develop an "intergenerational pact for the life of the Colombian Amazon ... to adopt measures aimed at reducing deforestation to zero".[40]

In the ground-breaking case of *Urgenda v State of the Netherlands*, all three levels of court concluded that the Dutch government's under-ambitious climate target was unlawful and ordered the government to increase its stringency. The 2015 decision of the District Court referenced Article 21 of the Dutch constitution (state obligation of environmental protection) in its holding, while the appellate and Supreme Court both based their judgements on the European Convention on Human Rights (ECHR), which is constitutionally entrenched in Dutch law.[41] In particular, the court sustained Urgenda's claim under Article 2 of the ECHR (right to life) and Article 8 of the ECHR (right to privacy and family life). The Court of Appeal, for example, held that climate change creates "the serious risk that the current generation of citizens will be confronted with loss of life and/or a disruption of family life" and therefore ECHR required the government to take meaningful action in accordance with the relevant science as elucidated by the Intergovernmental Panel on Climate Change (IPCC).[42]

In December of 2019, the Supreme Court of the Netherlands upheld the lower-court decisions in a strong decision recognising the state's human rights obligations in relation to climate change, despite its global nature, diffuse impacts and the problem of scientific uncertainty:

> [Dangerous climate change] entails the risk that the lives and welfare of Dutch residents could be seriously jeopardised. The same applies to, *inter alia*, the possible sharp rise in the sea level, which could render part of the Netherlands uninhabitable. The fact that this risk will only be able to materialise a few decades from now and that it will not impact specific persons or a specific group of persons but large parts of the population does not mean – contrary to the State's assertions – that Articles 2 and 8 ECHR offer no protection from this threat.... This is consistent with the precautionary principle.... The mere existence of a sufficiently genuine possibility that this risk will materialise means that suitable measures must be taken.[43]

Of particular relevance to ecological constitutionalism, both the Court of Appeal and the Supreme Court rejected the state's arguments that judicial intervention in climate change policy was a constitutionally impermissible violation of the separation of powers. Indeed, the Supreme Court noted that the Court of Appeal's decision reflected the "fundamental rule of constitutional democracy" that courts may order government to fulfil its legal obligations. This line of reasoning will be highly transferable to constitutional climate cases around the world.

Following in the footsteps of *Urgenda*, the petitioners in *Friends of the Irish Environment v Government of Ireland* argued that Ireland's weak national mitigation policy violated fundamental rights under the Irish Constitution and the ECHR and contravened the statute under which it was enacted (the 2015 Climate Act). The High Court recognised an unwritten constitutional right to an environment consistent with human dignity but held that the mitigation plan could not be said to violate or threaten such a right. Bypassing the Court of Appeal, the matter was expedited to the Supreme Court which quashed the national mitigation plan, finding it *ultra vires* the 2015 Climate Act. Unfortunately, the Supreme Court overturned the High Court's recognition of an unwritten environmental right, though it left open the possibility that environmental conduct by the state could violate existing constitutional provisions.[44]

In 2020, in the Canadian case of *Mathur v Ontario*,[45] the courts recently refused to dismiss constitutional claims by a group of youths who argue that the provincial government's rollback of progressive climate targets violated their constitutional rights to life, liberty, security of the person and equality. As in *Urgenda*, the court rejected arguments that government climate policy was legally immune from constitutional review. For the first time in Canadian legal history, the court recognised that government climate policy could violate constitutional rights and held that the case should be resolved after a full analysis on the merits.

Most recently (at the time of writing), in *Association Oxfam France et al v France*, the administrative court in Paris held that France was liable for causing "prejudice éologique" (ecological harm) through inadequate measures to meet its greenhouse gas (GHG) targets. In coming to this conclusion, the court referenced both France's international law obligations (which have constitutional force in domestic French law) and the obligation to reduce or limit environmental impacts under the French *Charte de l'environnement*.

Although several constitutional climate cases have failed (thus far),[46] many more are working their way through domestic courts around the world alleging that government action and inaction on climate change violate a range of constitutionally guaranteed rights.[47] Litigants and civil society will continue to highlight the obvious interrelationship between climate change and constitutional rights, and this is emerging as a recognised best practice internationally.

The Special Rapporteur opines that "[a]pplying a rights-based approach clarifies the obligations of States and businesses; catalyses ambitious action; highlights the plight of the poorest and most vulnerable; and empowers people to become involved in designing and implementing solutions".[48] A rights-based approach also supports broad public participation in climate decision-making, including recognition of and respect for Indigenous traditional knowledge as part of the corpus of climate science and Indigenous legal systems as an important source of climate law.[49]

Equity considerations

Whether through textual inclusion or judicial interpretation, as constitutions begin to embrace climate protection, a crucial challenge will be the equitable allocation of the benefits and burdens of GHG emissions within and among nations. Locally or globally, communities that have benefited little from the economic activities responsible for climate change should not be disproportionately called upon to sacrifice their development to GHG reduction.[50] Moreover, all climate policies should be designed to protect, respect and fulfil human rights.[51] Indeed, constitutional guarantees of Indigenous rights and the rights to equality, life, liberty, personal security, water, health and dignity (among others) could act as a salutary guide for appropriate climate protection measures. In short,

> ...climate justice in the Anthropocene requires the promotion of a just transition to a sustainable future ... which at the same time protects the most vulnerable people and countries from the impact of anthropogenic climate change. There is much work here for constitutionalisation to do....[52]

Finally, since climate change is a quintessentially global problem, "states have an obligation to cooperate to achieve a low-carbon, climate resilient and sustainable future, which means sharing information; the transfer of zero-carbon, low-carbon and high-efficiency technologies from wealthy to less wealthy States [and] building capacity...".[53]

Notes

1 See Norbert Brunner et al., "The Human Right to Water in Law and Implementation" (2015) 4:3 Laws 413.
2 *Report of the Special Rapporteur on Human Rights and the Environment: Clean Air and the Right to a Healthy and Sustainable Environment*, OHCHR, 40th Session, UN Doc A/HRC/40/55 (2019).

3 Johan Rockström et al., "A Safe Operating Space for Humanity" (2009) 461 Nature 472; Johan Rockström et al., "Planetary Boundaries: Exploring the Safe Operating Space for Humanity" (2009) 14:2 Ecol Soc 32.

4 Will Steffen et al., "Planetary Boundaries: Guiding Human Development on a Changing Planet" (2015) 347:6223 Science 1259855-1 at 1259855-1 [Steffen et al., "Planetary Boundaries"].

5 *Ibid* at 1.

6 *Ibid.*

7 *Ibid* at 1259855-8.

8 See e.g. Duncan French and Louis J Kotzé, *Research Handbook on Law, Governance and Planetary Boundaries* (London: Edward Elgar, 2021); Louis J Kotzé and Rakhyun E Kim, "Earth System Law: The Juridical Dimensions of Earth System Governance" (2019) 1 Earth Syst Gov 100003.

9 See Louis J Kotzé, *Global Environmental Constitutionalism in the Anthropocene* (Oxford: Hart Publishing, 2016).

10 See Tiina Häyhä et al., "From Planetary Boundaries to National Fair Shares of the Safe Operating Space – How Can the Scales Be Bridged?" (2016) 40 Global Envtl Change 60.

11 Steffen et al., "Planetary Boundaries", *supra* note 4 at 1259855-4.

12 See Jonathan Verschuuren, "Climate Change" in Duncan French and Louis J Kotzé, eds, *Research Handbook on Law, Governance and Planetary Boundaries* (London: Edward Elgar, 2021) 245 at 259.

13 *Report of the Special Rapporteur on Human Rights and the Environment: Safe Climate*, OHCHR, UN Doc A/74/161 (2019) at para 26 [OHCHR, "Safe Climate"]. See also *Climate Change and Poverty: Report of the Special Rapporteur on Extreme Poverty and Human Rights*, OHCHR, 41st Session, A/HRC/41/39 (2019) at para 19; Louis J Kotzé, "The Anthropocene, Earth System Vulnerability and Socio-Ecological Injustice in an Age of Human Rights" (2019) 10:1 J Hum Rts Envtl 85.

14 *Constitution of the Dominican Republic* (13 June 2015) at art 194.

15 *Constitution of Viet Nam* (1 January 2014) at art 63.

16 *Constitution of Côte d'Ivoire* (8 November 2016); *Draft Constitution of Algeria* (1 November 2020).

17 *Constitution of the Kingdom of Thailand* (6 April 2017) at art 258(g)(1).

18 *Constitution of Cuba* (10 April 2019) at art 16.

19 *Constitution of (the Bolivarian Republic of) Venezuela* (20 December 1999) at art 127.

20 *Constitution of Zambia* (24 August 1991) at art 257.

21 *Constitution of Tunisia* (27 January 2014) at art 45.

22 *Constitution of 2008 of the Republic of Ecuador* (20 October 2008) at art 414.

23 *Ibid*, art 413.

24 *Ibid*, arts 406, 407, 409.

25 *Ibid*, art 276, para 4.

26 *Constitution of the Kingdom of Bhutan* (18 July 2008) at art 5, para 3.

27 *Report of the Special Rapporteur on the Issue of Human Rights Obligations Relating to the Enjoyment of a Safe, Clean, Healthy and Sustainable Environment*, OHCHR, 73rd Session, A/73/188 (2018) at para 43 [OHCHR, "Human rights obligations relating to the environment"].

28 *Asghar Leghari v Federation of Pakistan*, [2015] WP No 25501/2015 (Pakistan); *Asghar Leghari v Federation of Pakistan and* Others, [2018] PLD 2018 Lahore 364 (Pakistan) [*Asghar*, "2018"].
29 *Ibid* at para 11.
30 *Asghar*, "2018", *supra* note 28.
31 Emily Barritt and Boitumelo Sediti, "The Symbolic Value of *Leghari v Federation of Pakistan*: Climate Change Adjudication in the Global South" (2019) 30:2 King's College L Rev 203.
32 César Rodríguez-Garavito, "Beyond the Courtroom: The Impact of Judicial Activism on Socioeconomic Rights in Latin America" (2011) 89:7 Tex L Rev 1669.
33 *Ibid*; Emily Barrit and Sediti Boitumelo, "The Symbolic Value of *Leghari v Federation of Pakistan: Climate Change Adjudication in the Global South* (2019) 30:2 King's Law Journal 203.
34 *Ibid,* Barit and Boitumelo at 208.
35 See Louis J Kotzé and Anél Du Plessis, "Putting Africa on the Stand: A Bird's Eye View of Climate Change Litigation on the Continent" (2019) 50:3 Envtl L 615.
36 *Future Generations v Ministry of the Environment and Others*, [2018] STC4360-3018 (Colombia). See translation by Dejusticia, "Climate Change and Future Generations Lawsuit in Colombia: Key Excerpts from the Supreme Court's Decision" (13 April 2018), online: *Dejusticia* <www.dejusticia.org/en/climate-change-and-future-generations-lawsuit-in-colombia-key-excerpts-from-the-supreme-courts-decision/>.
37 *Ibid* at para 11.3.
38 *Ibid* at para 11.2.
39 *Ibid* at para 14.
40 *Ibid* at para 14.
41 *Urgenda Foundation v State of the Netherlands*, [2015] ECLI:NL: RBDHA:2015:7196 (Netherlands) [*Urgenda*, "District Court"]; [2018] ECLI:NL:GHDHA:2018:2610 (Netherlands) (*Urgenda*, Court of Appeal); [2019] ECLI:NL:HR:2019:2007 (Netherlands) [*Urgenda*, "Supreme Court"].
42 *Urgenda*, "Court of Appeal", *supra* note 41 at para 45.
43 *Urgenda*, "Supreme Court", *supra* note 41 at para 5.6.2.
44 *Friends of the Irish Environment v Government of Ireland*, [2017] 2017 No 793 JR (Ireland).
45 *Mathur v Ontario,* 2020 ONSC 6918; see also Nathalie Chalifour and Jessica Earle, "Feeling the Heat: Using the *Charter* to Take on Climate Change in Canada" (2018) 42 Vermont L Rev 689.
46 See generally Michael Burger et al., *Global Climate Change Litigation Report: 2020 Status Review* (Nairobi: United Nations Environment Programme, 2020).
47 *Ibid.*
48 OHCHR, "Safe Climate", *supra* note 13.
49 See e.g. Cuthbert C Makondo and David SG Thomas, "Climate Change Adaptation: Linking Indigenous Traditional Knowledge with Western Science for Effective Adaptation" (2018) 88 Envtl Sci Pol'y 83; Randall Abate and Elizabeth Ann Kronk, *Climate Change and Indigenous Peoples: The Search for Legal Remedies* (London: Edward Elgar, 2013).

50 Sumudu Atapattu, "Environmental Justice, Climate Justice and Constitutionalism: Protecting Vulnerable States and Communities" in Jordi Jaria-Manzano and Susana Borrás, eds, *Research Handbook on Climate Constitutionalism* (London: Edward Elgar, 2019) at 213–4.
51 OHCHR, "Safe Climate", *supra* note 13 at para 69.
52 Jordi Jaria-Manzano and Susana Borrás, eds, *Research Handbook on Climate Constitutionalism* (London: Edward Elgar, 2019) at 16.
53 OHCHR, "Human Rights Obligations Relating to the Environment", *supra* note 26 at para 68.

References

Abate, Randall & Elizabeth A Kronk, *Climate Change and Indigenous Peoples: The Search for Legal Remedies* (London: Edward Elgar, 2013).

Asghar Leghari v Federation of Pakistan, [2015] WP No 25501/2015 (Pakistan).

Asghar Leghari v Federation of Pakistan and Others, [2018] PLD 2018 Lahore 364 (Pakistan).

Atapattu, Sumudu, "Environmental Justice, Climate Justice and Constitutionalism: Protecting Vulnerable States and Communities" in Jordi Jaria-Manzano & Susana Borrás, eds, *Research Handbook on Climate Constitutionalism* (London: Edward Elgar, 2019) 195.

Barritt, Emily & Boitumelo Sediti, "The Symbolic Value of *Leghari v Federation of Pakistan*: Climate Change Adjudication in the Global South" (2019) 30:2 King's College L Rev 203.

Brunner, Norbert et al., "The Human Right to Water in Law and Implementation" (2015) 4:3 Laws 413.

Chalifour, Nathalie and Jessica Earle, "Feeling the Heat: Using the *Charter* to Take on Climate Change in Canada" (2018) 42 Vermont Law Review 689.

Climate Change and Poverty: Report of the Special Rapporteur on Extreme Poverty and Human Rights, OHCHR, 41st Sess, A/HRC/41/39 (2019).

Constitution of 2008 of the Republic of Ecuador (20 October 2008).

Constitution of Côte d'Ivoire (8 November 2016).

Constitution of Cuba (10 April 2019).

Constitution of (the Bolivarian Republic of) Venezuela (20 December 1999).

Constitution of the Dominican Republic (13 June 2015).

Constitution of the Kingdom of Bhutan (18 July 2008).

Constitution of the Kingdom of Thailand (6 April 2017).

Constitution of Tunisia (27 January 2014).

Constitution of Viet Nam (1 January 2014).

Constitution of Zambia (24 August 1991).

Dejusticia, "Climate Change and Future Generations Lawsuit in Colombia: Key Excerpts from the Supreme Court's Decision" (13 April 2018), online: *Dejusticia* <www.dejusticia.org/en/climate-change-and-future-generations-lawsuit-in-colombia-key-excerpts-from-the-supreme-courts-decision/>.

Draft Constitution of Algeria (1 November 2020).

French, Duncan & Louis J Kotzé, *Research Handbook on Law, Governance and Planetary Boundaries* (London: Edward Elgar, 2021).

Friends of the Irish Environment v Government of Ireland, [2017] 2017 No 793 JR (Ireland).

Future Generations v Ministry of the Environment and Others, [2018] STC4360-3018 (Colombia).

Häyhä, Tiina et al., "From Planetary Boundaries to National Fair Shares of the Safe Operating Space – How Can the Scales Be Bridged?" (2016) 40 Global Envtl Change 60.

Hoexter, Cora, "Judicial Policy Revisited: Transformative Adjudication in Administrative Law" (2008) 24:2 SAJHR 281.

Jaria-Manzano, Jordi & Susana Borrás, eds, *Research Handbook on Climate Constitutionalism* (London: Edward Elgar, 2019).

Kotzé, Louis J, "The Anthropocene, Earth System Vulnerability and Socio-ecological Injustice in an Age of Human Rights" (2019) 10:1 J Hum Rts Envtl 85.

Kotzé, Louis J, *Global Environmental Constitutionalism in the Anthropocene* (Oxford: Hart Publishing, 2016).

Kotzé, Louis J & Anél Du Plessis, "Putting Africa on the Stand: A Bird's Eye View of Climate Change Litigation on the Continent" (2019) 50:3 Envtl L 615.

Kotzé, Louis J & Rakhyun E Kim, "Earth System Law: The Juridical Dimensions of Earth System Governance" (2019) 1 Earth Syst Gov 100003.

Makondo, Cuthbert C & David SG Thomas, "Climate Change Adaptation: Linking Indigenous Traditional Knowledge with Western Science for Effective Adaptation" (2018) 88 Envtl Sci Pol'y 83.

Mathur v Ontario, 2020 ONSC 6918.

Report of the Special Rapporteur on the Issue of Human Rights Obligations Relating to the Enjoyment of a Safe, Clean, Healthy and Sustainable Environment, OHCHR, 73rd Sess, A/73/188 (2018)

Report of the Special Rapporteur on Human Rights and the Environment: Clean Air and the Right to a Healthy and Sustainable Environment, OHCHR, 40th Sess, UN Doc A/HRC/40/55 (2019).

Report of the Special Rapporteur on Human Rights and the Environment: Safe Climate, OHCHR, UN Doc A/74/161 (2019).

Rockström, Johan et al., "A Safe Operating Space for Humanity" (2009) 461 Nature 472.

Rockström, Johan et al., "Planetary Boundaries: Exploring the Safe Operating Space for Humanity" (2009) 14:2 Ecol Soc 32.

Rodríguez-Garavito, César, "Beyond the Courtroom: The Impact of Judicial Activism on Socioeconomic Rights in Latin America" (2011) 89:7 Tex L Rev 1669.

Steffen, Will et al., "Planetary Boundaries: Guiding Human Development on a Changing Planet" (2015) 347:6223 Science 1259855-1 at 1259855-1.

Urgenda Foundation v State of the Netherlands, [2015] ECLI:NL: RBDHA:2015:7196 (Netherlands).

Urgenda Foundation v State of the Netherlands, [2018] ECLI:NL: GHDHA:2018:2610 (Netherlands).

Urgenda Foundation v State of the Netherlands, [2019] ECLI:NL:HR: 2019:2007 (Netherlands).

Verschuuren, Jonathan, "Climate Change" in Duncan French & Louis J Kotzé, eds, *Research Handbook on Law, Governance and Planetary Boundaries* (London: Edward Elgar, 2021) 245.

8 Conclusion

When I was a little girl spending summers in the glorious Canadian woods of southern Ontario, my mother told me many times to "respect the lake", "respect the river", "respect the forest". As much as my parents adored nature and took pains to expose me to it, this was also a warning. The understanding being imparted was that nature is more powerful than we are and if we want to thrive in a natural environment (and in the end there is no other kind), then we need to learn about and adapt ourselves to the dynamic characteristics of the natural world. You do not go near the water until you have learned to swim; you take a life jacket when going out in the canoe; and sometimes the signs of emerging bad weather require a change of plans. In short, our own human constructs need to take account of, and to *accommodate*, the demands of nature – not the other way around.

In the ecological paradigm that must emerge as a dominant framework for life in the Anthropocene, the legitimacy of human-made laws should be measured by the extent to which they comport with the inescapable laws of nature. Thus, ecological principles should be incorporated into the non-derogable laws of nations, i.e. constitutions. This transformation is necessary for the preservation of the natural world (including humanity), but also for the preservation of constitutions themselves. Without an ecological consciousness, the constitution is a paper temple – an aspirational blueprint for political community with no real guarantee of its survival over time. Ecological constitutionalism would "shift the environment from the periphery to the centre of constitutions"[1] and provide human societies with a powerful catalyst for change.

As the United Nations Special Rapporteur on Human Rights and the Environment has explained, "Transformative change requires rethinking the goals of society, what makes us happy and what it means to live a good life, how we generate and use energy, the food that we eat and how we produce it, the way that we man-ufacture goods, how we design our cities and how we can reduce and eliminate waste".[2] No single tool, legal or otherwise, can alone accomplish such a broad and deep transformation. But constitu-tions have a superordinate importance in the governance, politics and social consciousness of a nation. An ecological constitution – one that makes a serious, science-based attempt to sustain natural systems (including human communities) over time – could play a pivotal role in re-orienting our societies.

This book has argued that, at a minimum, an ecological approach to constitutionalism would codify: the principle of sustainability; the human right to "a safe, clean, healthy and sustainable envi-ronment";[3] the doctrines of intergenerational equity and the pub-lic trust; rights of nature; the precautionary principle; and rights and obligations relating to a healthy climate. The incorporation of some or all of these principles in domestic constitutions around the world would be a huge step in the journey towards sustainability. However, the efficacy of an ecological constitution (like all law) will depend entirely on its implementation by all branches of the state. The realisation of ecological constitutionalism hinges on the rule of law generally and the "environmental rule of law" in particular.[4] In short, we need a "rule of law for nature".[5] Thus, ecological gov-ernance is a crucial dimension of ecological law (and vice versa).[6]

Jeffords and Gellers underline the importance of effective gov-ernance mechanisms, and note the existence of some important exemplars from multiple regions around the world.[7] Several Latin American countries, for example, empower public officials to de-fend environmental rights, and these powers have been widely used.[8] In the Philippines, the Supreme Court has created a "writ of nature" to expedite hearings on serious violations of constitu-tional environmental rights;[9] and Ecuador's constitution empow-ers humans to defend not only their own environmental rights but also the rights of nature.[10] Because environmental matters often raise complex and contested scientific issues, there is also a need for judicial education in ecological literacy[11] and/or the constitutional creation of specialised environmental courts.[12]

Most importantly, however, constitutionalisation of ecological law has the potential to result in a "whole-of-government" approach to sustainability, as recommended by Woolley in her comprehensive and compelling analysis of ecological governance.[13] Since govern-ments routinely screen law and policy for constitutional compli-ance, there is reason to hope that the inclusion of robust ecological

protection in constitutions would awaken awareness and inspire action in multiple fields and at multiple levels of governance. Nothing
less will accomplish the necessary changes.

Some may question whether the adoption and implementation
of ecological constitutionalism is a realistic possibility given current global development trajectories. Building an ecological constitution is undoubtedly an exercise in optimism. But optimism is
at the heart of ecological law; indeed, it is a critical element of all
environmental activism.[14] The most powerful transformations in
human history have been accomplished by those who shared a positive, ambitious vision of a future far different from the present.[15]
In my view, ecological constitutionalism is one important pathway
from our present (unsustainable) environmental law regimes to a
future of robust, scientifically literate ecological law.[16] An ecological approach to constitutionalism could re-ground humans in the
real world, legally enshrine our innate love and respect for nature,[17]
and reanimate an enlightened survival instinct that could inspire
humanity to care for the complex web of life in which we are inex-
tricably embedded.

Notes

1 Klaus Bosselmann, *The Principle of Sustainability: Transforming Law
and Governance*, 2nd ed (London: Routledge, 2016) at 166.
2 *Report of the Special Rapporteur on the Issue of Human Rights Obligations in Relation to the Enjoyment of a Safe, Clean, Healthy and Sustainable Environment: Human Rights Depend on a Healthy Biosphere*,
OHCHR, 75th Sess, UN Doc A/75/161 (2020) at para 29 [OHCHR,
"Human Rights Depend on a Healthy Biosphere"]. See also Heather
McLeod-Kilmurray, "Does the Rule of Ecological Law Require Veganism? Ecological Law, Interspecies Justice and the Global Food System" (2019) 43 Vermont L Rev 455.
3 OHCHR, "Human Rights Depend on a Healthy Biosphere", *supra*
note ii.
4 Carl Bruch et al, *Environmental Rule of Law: First Global Report* (Nairobi: United Nations Environment Program, 2019).
5 Christina Voigt, *A Rule of Law for Nature: New Dimensions and Ideas
in Environmental Law* (Cambridge: Cambridge University Press, 2013).
6 See Olivia Woolley, *Ecological Governance: Reappraising Law's Role in
Protecting Ecosystem Functionality* (Cambridge: Cambridge University
Press, 2014).
7 Chris Jeffords & Joshua C Gellers, "Constitutionalizing Environmental Rights: A Practical Guide" (2017) 9:1 J Hum Rts Prac 136 at 141 [Jef-
fords & Gellers, "Constitutionalizing Environmental Rights"]; James
R May, "The Case for Environmental Human Rights: Recognition,

Implementation and Outcomes" (2021) Cardozo L Rev (forthcoming) [May, "The Case for Environmental Human Rights"].

8 See e.g. David R Boyd, *The Environmental Rights Revolution: A Global Study of Constitutions, Human Rights, and the Environment* (Vancouver: University of British Columbia Press, 2012) at 69 [Boyd, "The Environmental Rights Revolution"]. See also May, "The Case for Environmental Human Rights", *supra* note vii.

9 Hilario G Davide Jr, "The Environment as Life Sources and the Writ of Kalikasan in the Philippines" (2012) 29:2 Pace Envtl L Rev 592.

10 See Craig M Kauffman & Pamela L Martin, "Can Rights of Nature Make Development More Sustainable? Why Some Ecuadorian Cases Succeed and Others Fail" (2017) 92 World Dev 130.

11 See e.g. James R May & Erin Daly, *Judicial Handbook on Environmental Constitutionalism* (Nairobi: United Nations Environment Program, 2017).

12 United Nations Environment Programme, *Environmental Rule of Law: First Global Report*, UNEP, 2019, 1 at 202–10; Jeffords & Gellers, "Constitutionalizing Environmental Rights", *supra* note vii at 141.

13 Olivia Woolley, *Ecological Governance: Reappraising Law's Role in Protecting Ecosystem Functionality* (Cambridge: Cambridge University Press, 2014).

14 David R Boyd, *The Optimistic Environmentalist: Progressing toward a Greener Future* (Toronto: ECW Press, 2015); Lynda Collins & Brandon Stewart, "Engendering Hope in Environmental Law Students" in Amanda Kennedy et al, eds, *Teaching and Learning in Environmental Law: Pedagogy, Methodology and Best Practice* (Cheltenham: Edward Elgar, 2021).

15 Susan M Koger et al, "Climate Change: Psychological Solutions and Strategies for Change" (2011) 3:4 Ecopsychology 227 at 228 (internal citations omitted); David R Boyd, *The Rights of Nature: A Legal Revolution That Could Save the World* (Toronto: ECW Press, 2017) at 220–1.

16 See Kirsten Anker et al, *From Environmental to Ecological Law* (Abingdon: Routledge, 2021).

17 See generally Edward O Wilson, *Biophilia* (Cambridge, MA: Harvard University Press, 1984).

References

Anker, Kirsten et al, *From Environmental to Ecological Law* (Abingdon: Routledge, 2021).

Bosselmann, Klaus, *The Principle of Sustainability: Transforming Law and Governance*, 2nd ed (London: Routledge, 2016).

Boyd, David R, *The Environmental Rights Revolution: A Global Study of Constitutions, Human Rights, and the Environment* (Vancouver: University of British Columbia Press, 2012).

Boyd, David R, *The Optimistic Environmentalist: Progressing Toward a Greener Future* (Toronto: ECW Press, 2015).

Boyd, David R, *The Rights of Nature: A Legal Revolution That Could Save the World* (Toronto: ECW Press, 2017).

Bruch, Carl et al, *Environmental Rule of Law: First Global Report* (Nairobi: United Nations Environment Program, 2019).

Collins, Lynda M & Brandon Stewart, "Engendering Hope in Environmental Law Students" in Amanda Kennedy et al, eds, *Teaching and Learning in Environmental Law: Pedagogy, Methodology and Best Practice* (Cheltenham: Edward Elgar, forthcoming).

Davide Jr, Hilario G, "The Environment as Life Sources and the Writ of Kalikasan in the Philippines" (2012) 29:2 Pace Envtl L Rev 592.

Jeffords, Chris & Joshua C Gellers, "Constitutionalizing Environmental Rights: A Practical Guide" (2017) 9:1 J Hum Rts Prac 136.

Kauffman, Craig M & Pamela L Martin, "Can Rights of Nature Make Development More Sustainable? Why Some Ecuadorian Cases Succeed and Others Fail" (2017) 92 World Dev 130.

Koger, Susan M et al, "Climate Change: Psychological Solutions and Strategies for Change" (2011) 3:4 Ecopsychology 227.

May, James R, "The Case for Environmental Human Rights: Recognition, Implementation and Outcomes" (2021) 42 Cardozo L Rev 101.

May, James R & Erin Daly, *Judicial Handbook on Environmental Constitutionalism* (Nairobi: United Nations Environment Program, 2017).

McLeod-Kilmurray, Heather, "Does the Rule of Ecological Law Require Veganism? Ecological Law, Interspecies Justice and the Global Food System" (2019) 43 Vermont L Rev 455.

Report of the Special Rapporteur on the Issue of Human Rights Obligations in Relation to the Enjoyment of a Safe, Clean, Healthy and Sustainable Environment: Human Rights Depend on a Healthy Biosphere, OHCHR, 75th Sess, UN Doc A/75/161 (2020).

United Nations Environment Programme, *Environmental Rule of Law: First Global Report*, UNEP, 2019, 1.

Voigt, Christina, *A Rule of Law for Nature: New Dimensions and Ideas in Environmental Law* (Cambridge: Cambridge University Press, 2013).

Wilson, Edward O, *Biophilia* (Cambridge, MA: Harvard University Press, 1984).

Woolley, Olivia, *Ecological Governance: Reappraising Law's Role in Protecting Ecosystem Functionality* (Cambridge: Cambridge University Press, 2014).

Index

For Product Safety Concerns and Information please contact our EU
representative GPSR@taylorandfrancis.com
Taylor & Francis Verlag GmbH, Kaufingerstraße 24, 80331 München, Germany